HORSE

GOAT

MONKEY

Your capacity for hard work is amazing. You are your own person—very independent. While intelligent and friendly, you have a strong streak of selfishness and sharp cunning and should guard against being egotistical. Your sign suggests success as an adventurer, scientist, poet, or politician. Some Horses: Genghis Khan, Rembrandt, Chopin, Davy Crockett, Roger Ebert, Teddy Roosevelt.

Except for the knack of always getting off on the wrong foot with people, the Goat can be charming company. You are elegant and artistic but the first to complain about things. Put aside your pessimism and worry and try to be less dependent on material comforts. You would be best as an actor, gardener, or beachcomber. Some Goats: Spartacus, Michelangelo, Rudolph Valentino, Mark Twain, Buckminster Fuller, Orville Wright.

You are a very intelligent and a very clever wit. Because of your extraordinary nature and magnetic personality, you are always well-liked. The Monkey, however, must guard against being an opportunist and distrustful of other people. Your sign promises success in any field you try. Some Monkeys: Julius Caesar, da Vinci, Harry S. Truman, Sharif, Elizabeth Taylor.

ROOSTER

DOG

PIG

The Rooster is a hard worker; shrewd and definite in decision making, often speaking his mind. Because of this, you tend to seem boastful to others. You are a dreamer, flashy dresser, and extravagant to an extreme. Born under this sign you should be happy as a restaurant owner, publicist, soldier, or world traveler. Some Roosters: Rudyard Kipling, Caruso, Adam Smith, Groucho Marx, Peter Ustinov.

The Dog will never let you down. Born under this sign you are honest, and faithful to those you love. You are plagued by constant worry, a sharp tongue, and a tendency to be a fault finder, however. You would make an excellent businessman, activist, teacher, or secret agent. Some Dogs: Socrates, George Gershwin, Benjamin Franklin, Herbert Hoover, David Niven.

You are a splendid companion, an intellectual with a very strong need to set difficult goals and carry them out. You are sincere, tolerant, and honest but by expecting the same from others, you are incredibly naïve. Your quest for material goods could be your downfall. The Pig would be best in the arts as an entertainer, or possibly a lawyer. Some Pigs: Albert Schweitzer, Meatloaf, Ernest Hemingway, Bronson Pinchot.

These Chinese astrological readings come from the Peking Gourmet Inn placemat.

MISSION STREET FOOD

MCSWEENEY'S
INSATIABLES

A note from the authors: A portion of the proceeds from the sale of this book go to supporting
Slow Food USA. Mission Street Food operated on a tight budget, characterized by low prices and the
donation of all of our profits to charitable causes. Too often, that resulted in the use of ingredients which
were not local, sustainable, organic, or responsibly sourced. While we do not regret our prioritization of
moral imperatives, we sincerely desire progressive reform of the American food system.

Slow Food USA works to "ensure equity, sustainability, and pleasure in the food we eat," and in spite of
MSF's bravado regarding fast-food fried chicken, we support their efforts. Who says you can't buy salvation?

For more information about McSweeney's, see *mcsweeneys.net*
For more information about Slow Food USA, see *slowfoodusa.org*
For additional Mission Street Food recipes, see *foodandwine.com/mission-street-food*

Front cover placemat courtesy of Peking Gourmet Inn.
Bulldog drawing by Walter Green.
Back cover photos by Alanna Hale.

McSweeney's and colophon are registered trademarks of McSweeney's Publishing.

ISBN: 978-1-936365-15-9

MISSION STREET FOOD

Recipes and Ideas from an Improbable Restaurant

**ANTHONY MYINT &
KAREN LEIBOWITZ**

CONTENTS

FOREWORD

In October 2008, I was working as the editor of *Eater SF*—the Bay Area arm of a national food and restaurant blog. One Thursday afternoon, I got a tip that a local line cook would be subletting a Guatemalan taco truck that night and selling souped-up sandwiches from it. Actually, the first line of the email (from a friend of Anthony Myint and Karen Leibowitz) was "High-falootin' line cook from Bar Tartine goes all nitty gritty and shit."

The idea was intriguing enough. As someone who spends his professional life trying to give the restaurant world a narrative, it was nice to have a built-in story—and a good one at that. There wasn't any precedent for this sort of endeavor in San Francisco—restaurant food was served in restaurants, and the city's "street food" was pretty much limited to hot dogs and tacos. I posted the relevant info and planned on making a trip out to see Mission Street Food for myself.

I didn't expect to encounter throngs of people waiting on a random darkened corner in the Mission District for an unknown line cook to serve them dinner from a roach coach. But lo and behold, there they were—and they would return in greater numbers the next week, and again the week after that. And after the fourth week? For reasons you'll read about in this book, the truck was shuttered. But the vision of Mission Street Food carried on.

Like Mission Street Food itself, this book is difficult to explain. It involves a recounting of an improbable story, some recipes, and above all, ideas. Whether or not you dined at Mission Street Food, or will ever dine at any of the restaurants that it spawned, this book conveys a sense of the quirkiness, the transience, the aspirations, and the thoughtfulness that characterize the endeavor.

The influence of MSF is impossible to assess. To say that its fleeting, weeks-long taco-truck popularity inaugurated a citywide interest in street food would probably be an overstatement. To suggest that its biweekly dinners inside a Chinese restaurant foreshadowed the widespread appearance of pop-up restaurants is, well, debatable. To point to its use of social media, guest-chef appearances, and charitable agenda as iconoclastic is only partially accurate. But as a food writer, I appreciate Mission Street Food's story. As a professional eater, I'm a diehard fan of their cooking and its point of view. And as part of the local community, I appreciate its charitable angle, which broadened our discussion of the tricky politics of eating. I guess what I'm trying to say is that while it's impossible to gauge the exact impact Mission Street Food has had on our city, it's also impossible to imagine the San Francisco food scene without it.

—*Paolo Lucchesi*
San Francisco Chronicle columnist

FROM THE DESK OF
ANTHONY MYINT AND KAREN LEIBOWITZ

Mission Street Food Business Plan

Executive Summary

The goal of Mission Street Food (hereafter **The Restaurant**) is to offer unpredictable eating experiences that make no profit, lose no money, and require a substantial amount of work. The Restaurant will serve a different menu every night, making it impossible to achieve any economies of scale or regular routines, resulting in food waste and short tempers.

Business Concept

The Restaurant will be a moderately priced, low-service restaurant offering dinner and ultra-non-premium beer once or twice a week.

The Restaurant will rely on guest workers (hereafter **Complete Strangers**) to prepare large volumes of food and coordinate staffing with no guarantee of compensation. The Restaurant's management team (hereafter **The Management**) will not test the Complete Strangers' food for quality prior to service. Another restaurant will simultaneously use the resources available to The Restaurant at all times.

The Management will allow Complete Strangers to determine the type of cuisine and the majority of the menu before making any plans for the week. This will necessitate occasionally sourcing produce or ingredients from extremely expensive purveyors (*see section titled "Unprofitable Agenda"*). Cooks familiar with The Restaurant's cooking equipment will not use that equipment, and will allow Complete Strangers to use it instead.

The style of service will vary in professionalism. Staff will not be required to have any experience, and will be allowed to work while under the influence of mind-altering substances if they so choose. Staff will be given the option of foregoing hourly compensation.

The ambiance will be "unsophisticated," and will be geared toward making customers "have difficulty seeing and hearing." The Restaurant's ambiance is expected to contribute to the creation of a devoted following of repeat customers who order large amounts of food.

The dinner menu will typically consist of plates ranging from $5 to $16, and diners will each be expected to order two to five plates. The Restaurant will associate itself with a category of food that is generally prepared with low-quality ingredients on public thoroughfares by purveyors who can disappear quickly in the event of food poisoning. The Restaurant is expected to compete favorably with a nearby Mexican restaurant serving some of the most gratifying food available in San Francisco for $7 per person.

INTRODUCTION

Mission Street Food is gone. It was a phenomenon of its time and place, an artifact of twenty-first-century San Francisco. But its story begins with a young man named Tan Houk Cho, who bore the stamp of his own time and place, far from contemporary American epicureanism.

Houk Cho came of age as a refugee, hiding in the jungle outside Rangoon with his mother and six siblings after the Japanese invaded Burma during World War II. When the war ended, his brothers and sisters went back to regular teenage things like school and dating, but Houk Cho was determined to support his mother and family, so that they could move out of the abandoned train car in which they had taken shelter. Houk Cho began his career as a lowly *chai-wallah*,[1] but quickly became a diplomat's assistant, then a gray-market document fabricator, and eventually the owner of a candy factory.

When Houk Cho was twenty-nine, the military staged a coup and seized control of the country; a series of increasingly discriminatory laws targeting the Chinese minority prompted our man to change his name to U Kyaw Myint, a typical Burmese name. Eventually, he married and made his way to the United States by way of two years of indentured servitude in an Australian coal mine and a covert taxi ride across the Canadian border. As a middle-aged man, U Kyaw changed his name again, to Victor Myint, and started from scratch once more, working his way up from dishwasher to business owner to day-trader—in spite of losing his right leg in a car accident soon after arriving in America.

Victor raised two children with his wife, Ellen, who became a successful entrepreneur in her own right. Inspired by an immigrant's thrift and folk-Buddhist notions of karma, Victor liked to buy the fruit that his local grocery store had deemed too old to sell, and then hand it out to homeless people at soup kitchens in Washington, D.C. While Victor's intent was noble, his son Anthony learned that the bananas were not welcome, and his father was known as "the crazy man who gets into shouting matches with homeless people over half-rotten fruit."[2] Anthony tried to discourage his father's idiosyncratic philanthropy, but Victor just dismissed him as "Mr. Know-All." Of course, this was a distortion of the American idiom, "know-it-all," but Anthony couldn't correct his father, because doing so would reinforce the nickname.

---

[1] A boy or young man who sells or serves tea, often at train stations or in other public spaces.

[2] Anthony gleaned this information from a former classmate who volunteered at the shelter. Incidentally, the classmate later developed schizophrenia and insisted he was part of both the Kennedy and Bush families.

Victor also enjoyed giving strangers photocopies of his own motivational slogans and political manifestos. As an old man, Victor liked to share his wisdom with anyone who would listen. These marathon lectures invariably opened with the phrase, "Can I tell you something?" and featured diagrams and zoological metaphors illustrating his personal history and life lessons. For example: "A monkey standing under a fruit tree cannot starve. If you are in the United States, you cannot be broke."

In the end, Victor's selflessness was matched only by his stubbornness. He became increasingly crotchety, even as his life became ever more American and suburban. He and Ellen divorced, and their children moved away. He had sponsored his extended family's immigration to the U.S. over the years, but at the end of his life, Victor lived alone with his memories and CNN. His high blood pressure led to further health problems, and Victor passed away in 2009, shortly before his seventy-fifth birthday.

In this capsule of a life's story are the principles that set the table for Mission Street Food: willfulness, naiveté, resourcefulness, altruism, moral flexibility, putative insanity, and a compulsion to use food efficiently.

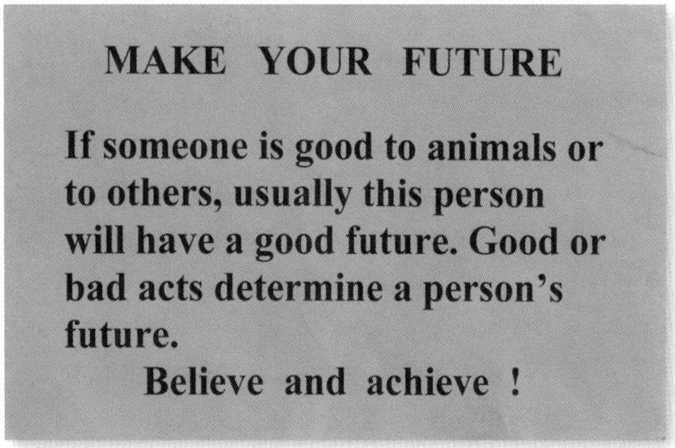

MAKE YOUR FUTURE

If someone is good to animals or to others, usually this person will have a good future. Good or bad acts determine a person's future.
Believe and achieve !

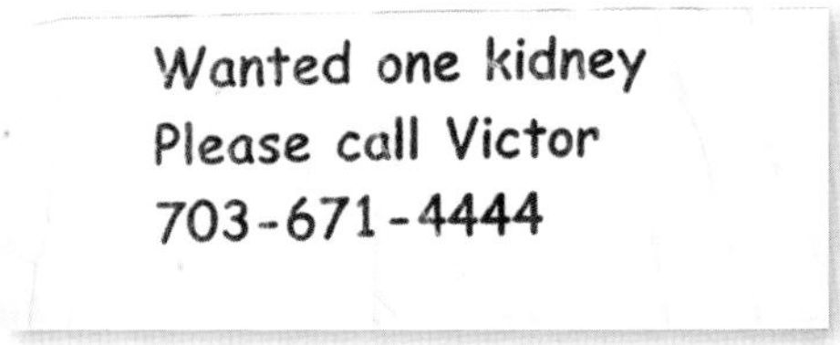

Wanted one kidney
Please call Victor
703-671-4444

**VICTOR MYINT'S
HOMEMADE FLYERS**

In his later years, Anthony's father would craft motivational posters, and share advice with anyone who would listen.

PART ONE

THE TACO TRUCK

Anthony's idea of leisure usually involves a lot of work, so this promised to be another one of his idiosyncratic larks.

ANTHONY: I'm my father's son, for better or worse. The house where I grew up, in suburban Northern Virginia, served as the administrative headquarters for All Service Corporation, my father's gas-station-repair business. He always pushed me academically, so I could avoid the kind of hardships he had endured. I attended one of the nation's top high schools, graduated from a good liberal-arts college with a degree in Economics and Asian Studies, and found a low-paying job surfing the web at a market-research firm. I couldn't exactly say I was fulfilling my parents' American dream.

When my mom and dad separated in 1999, I moved in with my dad because it seemed like he needed some company. After a few years of aimless office work, I had saved $10,000, which I spent on a six-month world tour spanning thirty countries on six continents. The trip was ostensibly for fun rather than self-discovery—I went with my friend Dennis Kim—but the experience really did change me. I saw incredible poverty in India and unbelievable wealth in Dubai; I marveled at Buddhist monks in Lhasa and ladyboys in Bangkok; I tasted street food in Eastern Europe and East Africa and East Asia. Maintaining a tight budget required considerable ingenuity and flexibility, but our first-world resourcefulness paled in comparison to that of the matatu drivers of Uganda, the tailors/pimps of Vietnam, or the llama herders of the

THE MYINT FAMILY
(Above) Victor, Vicky, Anthony, and Ellen.

MSF'S FOUNDERS

Anthony Myint and Karen Leibowitz.

Bolivian salt flats. Though I never made it to Burma, I got a better sense of where my parents came from.

Back in suburban Virginia, things seemed smaller and plainer than ever—especially the food. It didn't matter if I was at a fast-food chain or a local ethnic joint; I would always wonder why restaurants didn't serve better food when it was so obvious how they could improve. Finally, after a few months of acting like a real Mr. Know-All, I decided to become a cook, and maybe someday a restaurant owner who would do it right.

I dreamed of a restaurant that would combine my favorite American foods with the best things I'd tasted during my travels. I even wrote up a business plan for an "Asian soul food" restaurant, which I wanted to call Umami, after the Japanese term for the savory fifth flavor. (Western science had recently confirmed that the human tongue has receptors for *umami*, in addition to those for salty, sweet, sour, and bitter. There are also receptors for a sixth flavor, astringent, and even a lone receptor dedicated to sensing water.)

My Asian soul food concept seemed like it might work better in a big city, particularly one with a large Asian-American population, so I moved to San Francisco. When I arrived in the Bay Area in April 2004, I stayed with two high-school friends who were sharing an apartment in Berkeley with a graduate student. During the first few weeks of my new life, I slept on their couch, looked for my first restaurant job, and fell in love with their roommate, Karen Leibowitz.

KAREN: When I met Anthony, I was completing my doctorate in English literature at UC Berkeley. I'd become close friends with my roommates, Simon Huynh and Eli Horowitz, so it was easy to feel like I already knew Anthony and the world he'd come from. At first, our friends were surprised to see us becoming a couple, because we seemed so different. I was gregarious while Anthony was shy; I was a big reader while he was a sports fan; I was a woman while he'd never really talked to one before.

But at heart, we're similar in the ways that count. We value rationality and quirkiness in equal measure, so it's easy for us to make joint decisions and to make each other laugh. In the summer of 2005, after about a year of dating, we got engaged and moved in together in the Mission District of San Francisco. While setting up our apartment, we naturally started talking about our plans for the future, and Anthony asked me, "How much money do you think we should try to have?" I didn't think we needed too much. As a graduate student, I was used to living simply, and with Anthony cooking for me, my life already seemed rich.

Anthony explained that he wanted to start a restaurant that functioned like a non-profit—with employees taking salaries, but additional proceeds going to worthy causes. "Asian soul food" had morphed into a "benevolent business."

For the next few years, we both pursued our educations, with me commuting to UC Berkeley and Anthony working in various San Francisco restaurants. We got married in 2007, with my former roommates Simon and Eli officiating the ceremony.

ANTHONY: By late 2008, I'd been working at a restaurant called Bar Tartine for three years. It was owned by the couple behind the renowned Tartine Bakery, and I'd advanced from prep cook to *garde manger* to lead line cook under the tutelage of a very accomplished chef named Jason Fox. I really liked the staff and the food we were serving, so I stayed on even though I knew that I'd learn more at a new job. I began thinking of ways to open a restaurant, without leaving Bar Tartine or taking any drastic risks. A few months later, I found the solution staring me in the face from the window of a Guatemalan snack cart.

Walking home from work on Friday and Saturday nights, I used to pass by a small trailer parked near the bars on Mission Street. Antojitos San Miguel was equipped with a tiny kitchen and a window facing the sidewalk, and it was literally a mom-and-pop business: Juanita took the orders, and her husband Gomez cooked. With less ceremony than one might expect,

I arranged to rent the cart on Thursday nights, my usual day off.

Karen and I could hang out on Mission Street while cooking and chatting together— a surrogate mom-and-pop business, if you will. We'd call it Mission Street Food.

KAREN: It's hard to remember how we thought about Mission Street Food before it existed. It certainly felt like it would be a hobby more than a business, but sometimes it bordered on a joke. Anthony really wanted to name our pork-belly sandwich the "Clean Sanchez," but I told him that he wouldn't want to explain that one to his parents.[3] He said they'd never have to know about it at all.

The whole taco-truck plan really seemed like another one of his quixotic projects. A few years earlier, he built a massive five-foot papier-mâché owl for Eli's birthday, and then proceeded to devise increasingly elaborate costumes for it each year thereafter. Anthony's idea of leisure usually involves a lot of work, so this promised to be another one of his idiosyncratic larks.

ANTHONY: We eventually called that sandwich the PB&J, and it really illustrates the importance of a good name. (Culinary entrepreneurs take note: people will try anything called a PB&J.) I was determined to use pork belly (the "PB"), because it's cheap and deli-

cious, and I eventually settled on marinated jicama (the "J") as an accompaniment while developing recipes in the weeks leading up to our first night. I enjoy the brightness of the pickled vegetables in Vietnamese *banh mi* sandwiches, which served as a reference point. But a "Pork Belly and Radish" sandwich has much less cultural cachet than a "PB&J." Besides, jicama's crisper and less funky-tasting than radish.

In addition to the PB&J (*see pages 133–135*), we decided on a flatbread sandwich featuring exotic mushrooms, which I love. Karen said we needed an iconic name—like the Big Mac—so we tried to evoke a similar grandeur with the King Trumpet. It had sautéed trumpet mushrooms, charred-scallion sour cream, garlic confit, and triple-fried potatoes (*see pages 164–166*). Our third sandwich was nothing more than a well-executed quesadilla (which is nothing to scoff at) with roasted pasilla peppers and avocado. We called it the Mission Melt for the sake of alliteration. Some names are better than others, alas.

At first, I was leaning toward serving the sandwiches on shallow-fried flour tortillas, but Jason and the cooks at Bar Tartine convinced me to devise my own recipe for flatbread (*see page 169*). I did, and for most of September 2008, the Bar Tartine kitchen served as a testing ground for countless iterations of the flatbread sandwiches that eventually became the signature dish of Mission Street Food.

---

3 This would have been a completely gratuitous reference to the "dirty Sanchez," since there is almost no connection between sandwiches and mustaches.

That kitchen was modest by restaurant standards, but resourceful cooks can do a lot with a little. The hot line had two ranges, a small gas grill, and a deep fryer manned by two cooks, plus one on the *garde manger* station. But under Jason's direction, we were capable of putting out incredible food—food on par with any restaurant in the city. In spite of the limited space, Jason good-naturedly allowed me to use his kitchen to supplement the truck's facilities (just a griddle and some unreliable refrigeration).

KAREN: At the time, we were enthralled by the "duck-shreds burrito" at Koi Palace, a dim sum powerhouse in a suburb of San Francisco. Much of their menu consists of excellent renditions of dim sum classics, but this item is a notable innovation. They wrap fresh scallion pancakes (*cong you bing*) around roasted duck meat and skin, along with hoisin, cilantro, and julienned cucumber. The flaky, oily wrapper takes Peking duck to the next level, so we decided to model our own sandwich wrappers on their delightful hybrid. After dropping the scallions and using butter instead of oil, the resulting flatbread looked like *chapati* and tasted like croissants.

ANTHONY: They also took about as much time to prepare as croissants. The process involves making dough; resting it; portioning it; rolling it out; applying butter, salt, and pepper; rolling it up into a cigar; stretching that tube; coiling it into a spiral; rolling that back out into a pancake; stacking the flatbreads on parchment; and plastic wrapping— a process that averaged about three minutes per

OWL VARIATIONS

Lucha libre owl, après-ski owl, hula owl.

KOI PALACE DIM SUM HIGHLIGHTS

(Opposite page) Duck-shreds burrito.

(Top to bottom): Cold seafood plate, soup dumplings, chicken rice porridge, zhaliang (Chinese donuts wrapped in rice sheets).

flatbread. For the first night in the truck, I made eighty flatbreads, and barely finished in time to go camp out for a parking space.

Opening night nerves are universal, but on most opening nights the chef has at least cooked in the kitchen. In this case, it was about three hours before opening and I didn't even have a place to park my kitchen yet. I was waiting for a couple of car owners to come back so I could snag their spaces for the food truck. (Legally, the Antojitos San Miguel cart could only sell food on the particular corner where I had first encountered it, because San Francisco has highly restrictive policies regarding street food.) Complicating matters was our need to hold both spaces with one car—I don't know how Gomez and Juanita pulled it off on a regular basis.

By 5:15, I'd only secured one spot, and with each passing minute, it became more likely that the holder of the second spot would not return at all. At 5:26, an elderly gentleman came to feed the meter. I asked politely if he would consider moving his car to a nearby space, offering to pay for his parking anywhere else. He said he was leaving at 6 p.m. anyway and walked back into a shop that sold knick knacks across the street. The waiting game continued.

At 6:07 I got impatient. With less than an hour before the truck's arrival, I went to look for the man in the Avalon Shop's clutter of T-shirts, hats, flags, and novelties and found him asleep in the back. Crucial minutes of prep were evaporating while the foolhardiness of my plan echoed with every snore. But then a young woman descended on the scene like an angelic social

A PARTIAL LIST OF MSF FLATBREAD SANDWICHES:

PB&J (pork belly, jicama, cilantro aioli, jalapeño)

King Trumpet (trumpet mushrooms, triple-fried potato, garlic confit, charred-scallion sour cream)

Mission Melt (Monterey Jack cheese, pasilla peppers, onion, avocado)

Peking Duck (duck confit, crispy skin, cucumber, spicy hoisin, cilantro)

Chicken-fried beef jerky with snap peas, shaved squash, and ranch dressing

BBBLT (braised Benton's bacon, lettuce, baked tomato, and smokehouse aioli)

Crab fritters, edamame purée, pickled hon shimeji mushroom, and nori crumble

Fried catfish, avocado, braised kimchi, and tamago

Lamb curry with seared peppers, fresh garbanzo, and cilantro yogurt on a garlic flatbread

Chicken with Forty Cloves (shredded chicken, garlic confit, shishito peppers, gremolata)

Lamb belly, chorizo, marinated beet, goat yogurt, and mache

Braised sausage, eggplant tempura, tomato reduction, goat cheese, and basil

Eel-banana tempura with blueberry-IPA compote and fried polenta

Gyro (lamb belly, spicy lamb meatballs, lamb merguez, with goat cheese tzatziki and pickled red onion)

Trotter flatbread (ham hock rillette, cornichon, sauce gribiche)

Corned beef, slow-cooked sauerkraut, Russian dressing, and Swiss on a rye flatbread

worker; she woke up gramps, diffused his grumpiness, and got him to re-park. I "reserved" the second spot with some "borrowed" utility-repair no-parking signs that I'd stashed in the trunk of our car, and frantically returned to last-minute prep.

When 7:00 came and went with no sign of Gomez, panic mounted again. But at 7:20, the hulking trailer rounded the corner from Mission Street, as glorious as a Hummer SUV on prom night. And then, amid a flurry of rearranging cars, trailers, and coolers full of food, Karen arrived.

KAREN: On the day of Mission Street Food's debut, I was teaching in Berkeley. As soon as my class ended, I raced back to the city, and then up Mission Street to our rendezvous point, only to find that a customer was already waiting expectantly while Anthony scrambled to get set up. I asked this stranger how he'd heard about us, and he said *Mission Mission* and *Eater SF*. I'd never heard of either website, but apparently they knew all about us, thanks to a big-mouthed friend named Chris Ying. I ran home to get our signs and bake off some cookies.

For someone with no interest in running restaurants, I was running a lot.

ANTHONY: By 8 p.m., the publicized start time, I could see a line forming down the block. Karen was baking cookies, and I was still organizing inside the truck. Gomez had left the refrigerators full of food and the cooking station full of sour cream and oxidizing avocados, leaving me no room whatsoever. I pulled a bunch of produce out of the fridge and piled some in the sink and some next to the fried chicken they'd kept out to serve again the next day. (Roach coach, indeed.) By 8:15, I had a pot of oil heating and a flatbread burning on the griddle. Karen came back and slapped up the laminated, magnetic signs we'd made at Kinko's, and we opened the window for business.

KAREN: When I came back to the truck with the cookies, there was already a formidable line. We were completely overwhelmed, and our plans were obviously useless. Instead of getting in the truck with Anthony, I worked my way down the line

RESTAURANT 2.0:
BRINGING ONLINE SOCIALITY TO THE STREETS

by Sang-hyoun Pahk, doctoral student of sociology and former manager of Mission Street Food

Karen and Anthony opened the first incarnation of Mission Street Food to the public at around 8 p.m. on October 2, 2008. Their opening was preceded by a "press release," penned by a friend, which was posted on a handful of local blogs early that afternoon:

TONIGHT (THURSDAY): High-falootin' line cook from Bar Tartine goes all nitty gritty and shit. Anthony Myint is subletting an antojitos truck in what, hopefully, will become a recurring Thursday night event. He'll be peddling an assortment of sandwiches, each served on a piece of homemade scallion flatbread. Among them, the highly anticipated PB&J (Pork Belly and Jicama) and the busty vegetarian King Trumpet (wild mushrooms and triple-fried potato).

WHEN: Thursday night, 8pm-2am. Watch Biden dispense of Palin and then hop down to 21st and Mission to still your beating heart. Um, prices are reasonable, dude. $3–$5. Support local line cooks.

Despite the obvious excitement, Anthony anticipated a "soft opening consisting of foot traffic and a couple of friends." Anonymous posters on Yelp were more skeptical ("He's going to park a roach coach on Mission and start selling food? I doubt it"; "21st and mission...don't wear red. don't wear blue. don't get shot. don't die. good speed"). And really, the skeptics were justified. Just a few months before, the *SF Weekly* had run a feature called "State of the Cart," the central premise of which was that while San Francisco was justifiably "famed as a gastronomic destination," it fell "perplexingly short" in terms of street food.[1]

What happened next, I think, took everyone by surprise. That night, Anthony and Karen opened up to a line of customers, sold out of food early, and then basically repeated that sequence each Thursday until they couldn't. Within about four weeks, Anthony and Karen had moved indoors, but they had been replaced outside by a small army of independent vendors peddling an incredible variety of street food in the Mission. By fall 2009, the phenomenon was drawing attention from elite institutions;[2] in February 2010, the *New York Times* ran an article on "Coming to Terms with a Street Food Boom" that detailed growing concerns from local officials and business owners about the "dozens of new licensed and unlicensed mobile vendors v[ying] for spaces at San Francisco's parks and sidewalks."[3]

So what happened? Why did Mission Street Food generate so much excitement on those Thursday nights? And why, in the summer of 2009, did so many other people decide to suddenly try their hand at selling food on the street, as if some kind of floodgate had been opened? One way of answering these questions is to ask the vendors themselves. And the answers they give make sense: Anthony noticed that the Antojitos truck was missing from its usual corner on his nights off; Brian (of the Magic Curry Kart) traveled to Thailand and was inspired; Kristen (of the Sexy Soup Cart) saw an opportunity to make healthy food more available. And why were they successful? Well, that can be explained, too. The food cart vendors I talked to generally came off as inventive, dedicated, and articulate about what they were doing. They had a strong sense of who their customers were and how to appeal to them, what obstacles existed and how to overcome them, and, of course, they were selling a pretty good product at very good prices. But then, why 2009 instead of 2007? Or 2001? And why all at once?

One approach is to look for "macro" reasons. One plausible explanation for the timing of the street-food boom is that it coincided with the recession. With fewer jobs available, some industrious people were pushed to seek alternative ways of making rent, while consumers were sent looking for cheaper alternatives to fine dining. This makes a lot of sense—but the recession didn't just drive customers to frequent the Mission's taco trucks. And generally speaking, the people involved in the new street-food scene were not among those hit hardest by the economic downturn. They were young, middle class, and mostly white.

So what explains their success? Unlike the hot dog carts and taco trucks that preceded them, new street carts were mobile and unpredictable. They didn't establish reliable hours and territory (at least at first). Instead, they used blogs to publicize their existence and Twitter to let customers know when and where they were selling. Social media made new street food ventures interesting (and possible). Without those first blog posts, MSF's first Thursday really

would have been "foot traffic and a couple of friends." The use of Twitter in conjunction with those blogs took things to a new level. Steven (of Gobba Gobba Hey) neatly summarized the impact of Twitter and blogs in his account of his first outing:

> *I tried to use Twitter to announce that I was going to be selling on the street, but of course no one was really following me so no one knew. I had exchanged emails with Murat of Amuse Bouche and fortuitously he emailed me the day that I was going to sell. He and his wife, Pelin, came out to meet me and then logged onto Twitter and talked about how much they enjoyed my food. The next day I suddenly had "followers" on Twitter, and SF Weekly's "Pavement Cuisine" columnist Tamara Palmer contacted me and asked if she could come over and do a taste testing. The paper ran a blurb online that evening. Suddenly I was "the new street food vendor" in SF.*

Of course, you can sell food on the streets without Twitter, but using Twitter let vendors do things they otherwise couldn't CONTINUED ON NEXT PAGE have. Unlike Anthony, most of the vendors didn't concern themselves with the various permits required to sell food legally, which can be prohibitively expensive and time-consuming.[4] And if they were asked to leave by neighbors or the police, Twitter allowed them to relocate without fear of leaving their customers behind.

This is the key innovation that enabled the flood of vendors that we saw in 2009, and also partly explains why we hadn't seen anything like it before—Twitter wasn't ready yet. But what explains the enthusiasm on diners' part that seemingly swept the Mission that summer? Why did people find hunting down crème brûlée on Twitter so exciting? Basically, what did it all mean? One (hyper-articulate) customer explained it to me this way:

> I think we are all desperately seeking some kind of connection in our consumptive behaviors. We're tired of being the alienated, atomized consumer. It's fun to talk to the guy whose cart it is. It's fun to talk to the other customers. We're in line for the same thing, I guess. It's like we exchanged our money for something more than just food. Like, why do people get excited about being a regular someplace, besides the possibility of freebies? There's a connection.

I think she's right. The Yelp pages of bacon-wrapped-hot-dog carts don't refer to the proprietors by their first names. And as far as I know, there's no shared sense of adventure or rebellion or anything else among people that wait in line for burritos.[5] But the new street-food phenomenon happened as much online as offline. This meant, among other things, that the "meaning" of street food was constructed on blog posts and in Twitter conversations rather than dictated by vendors. It became identified with adventure, community, and irony. In other words, what the vendors did resonated with consumers in part because the consumers made it that way through their participation online.

And in turn, some of the social logics and values that operate online found their way into the practices of the new street food. The openness and collaboration that we have come to understand as "naturally" part of sites like Wikipedia are also evident in new street food. And the hacker ethic (which includes repurposing of old tools to new uses and a playful disregard for existing boundaries) can be read as one of the foundational principles of the new street food.

But street food's close connection to social media had consequences as well. Because comfort with social media requires consistent Internet access and fluency in an online culture that is pretty specific (it helps to have a smart phone, too), new street food effectively excluded a large part of the neighborhood. From the outside, impromptu street food "fairs" put on by vendors looked a lot like upscale slow-food gatherings, despite the fact that street food had working-class-friendly prices. This is a reminder that social media isn't as predictable as we might sometimes imagine it to be.[6]

---

1 Meredith Brody. "State of the Cart." *SF Weekly*. July 16, 2008.

2 Including the Culinary Institute of America (Josh Harkinson. "Street Food Fight." *Mother Jones*. December 1, 2009) and the Commonwealth Club of California.

3 Tara Duggan. "Coming to Terms With a Street Food Boom." The *New York Times*. February 25, 2010.

4 Some activities, like cooking food for paying customers on make-shift burners, could not be licensed regardless. And, as it turned out, Anthony and Karen's "borrowed" licenses didn't keep them from getting pushed off their corner, anyway.

5 This is not to say that such things couldn't or didn't happen. But new street food was basically defined by these connections in a way that the traditional version is clearly not.

6 Consider, for example, the recent revelation that less than 15 percent of contributors to Wikipedia are women. Both the causes and consequences of this disparity are unclear, as are the ethical responsibilities of Wikipedia's stewards to either repair this imbalance or refrain from meddling. The pattern of exclusion evident in new street food is much less of a mystery.

selling cookies until someone pointed out that people don't like it when you take their money and serve them food with the same hand. A friend stepped in to distribute the cookies, while I took orders and collected money. Another friend (Chris Ying again) had already climbed into the truck to help Anthony cook.

It had never occurred to us that we might have more than a few customers at a time, so we had no system for organizing orders. On the fly, I decided to give each person a letter, which was a big mistake. A lot of letters sound the same, so I spent the night yelling things like "Order D! D as in Depeche Mode!" It was like taking a free-association test in front of a hundred people. I had no cash register, of course, so I kept ones and fives in my front pockets, tens and twenties in my back pockets—a regular carnie. And I kept running home to bake more cookies.

ANTHONY: Over the course of that night, a lot of things went wrong—food was slowly and sloppily assembled, I burned more than a few flatbreads, and we subbed in store-bought tortillas for the last hour—but a lot of things went right. We sold out of our whole menu, we pulled off a piecemeal and untested plan, and we received an enthusiastic response from our customers to an unconventional hybrid of street food and fine dining. These kinds of successes, surrounded by risk, frenzy, and mistakes,

would become routine over the course of MSF's run.

KAREN: By the end of the night, I started to calm down. Initially, I'd felt like I needed to charm people to distract them from the stupidity of standing in line for food, but in fact, the wait was so long that people started to have real conversations among themselves. When we ran out of flatbreads, a group of people went and got their own loaf of bread from the corner store, and one of them admitted that he had never liked fresh flatbread, even though his mother made her own naan every day. Everybody milled around chatting; I felt like a block captain.

ANTHONY: That night we went home and launched the Mission Street Food blog. We'd cleaned up the truck and returned the keys to Gomez around midnight; Karen and I were dog-tired and facing the prospect of a full week of work, along with the new obligation of predicting and meeting the demands of another MSF the next Thursday. We just needed a way to tell people what to expect if it rained, or something like that, and we didn't consider our "online presence" beyond a thirty-second discussion of the background color for our Blogger site.

KAREN: In addition to the ongoing logistical chaos, the second and third weeks were

also characterized by soul-crippling uncertainty. Was Mission Street Food just a passing fad from which fickle foodies would move on? Would our friends keep showing up to bail us out? Of the countless variables involved, how many would go wrong? And even if there were no serious mishaps, how long could we maintain such a time-consuming hobby? (MSF was definitely still just a hobby at this point.) Winter rain was approaching, and besides, we'd surely get mugged soon. Anthony and I planned to stop after four or five weeks at most.

ANTHONY: To our genuine surprise, the publicity continued to be as abundant as the crowds. One item on the *Eater SF* website included a "Crucial Update," which reported, "brownies were topped with brie and hazelnuts." This was an update to their own earlier coverage on our switch from cookies to brownies. Just for reference: the San Francisco Bay Area is a metropolitan area of seven million people and more than four thousand restaurants.

We learned that Internet food journalism tends to fan the flames of any story until it can run a feature on how "hot" the topic has become. To keep up with demand, we increased production about 50 percent each week: from 80 sandwiches the first week to 125 the second night and 180 the third night. We sold out each time.

KAREN: By our fourth night in the truck, we'd come a long way. We'd prepped 240 flatbreads for service, cookies had given way to "filthy rich" brownies, and we'd added a slaw of Asian pear, iceberg lettuce, and horseradish to the menu. We'd hired a second cook, and systems were in place, even in terms of parking.[4] We were refining our business, updating our blog, and finding our voices as co-authors of this thing we had created.

ANTHONY: But at 7:50 on that fourth night, with forty people queued up for Mission Street Food, a neighborhood real-estate bigwig—let's call him J.J. Vanguard—arrived in his convertible BMW and had a full-on tantrum, screaming that we weren't allowed to be there, that we were leaving trash in front of his building, that we'd had this conversation before, and that he was going to call the cops.

KAREN: He definitely set off my fight-or-flight instincts: my pulse was beating in my ears and my knees felt wobbly. After his opening salvo, he stormed back to his car. I followed him to try to have a less confrontational conversation, but he immediately engaged me in a lunatic death-match over the soul of the Mission (i.e., which of us identified with taquerías more). Señor Vanguard resented hipsters coming in and making a mess, while I resented high-strung businessmen gracing our presence with their manic outbursts. We locked horns a while longer, then I went back to the truck.

---

4 **ANTHONY**: No thanks to a dickhead valet from a nearby restaurant who stole my spot as our truck was pulling in, then shrugged it off and ran away.

ANTHONY: It seemed unthinkable to just call it a night, disappoint the crowd, and waste all of the food, so we started cooking as fast as we could. The police eventually came—multiple times, in fact—to check the permits and give out a few tickets to people drinking from brown bags, just for good measure.

KAREN: That night, I was persecuted through my dreams by J.J. Vanguard and the pulsing vein in his forehead. He called me many times the next day, and my heart raced with fear each time I saw his number. I didn't answer the phone. Eventually, his personal assistant left me a voicemail saying that our permit only covered fruit and ice cream, so the police would be back to shut us down if we continued to cook. Whether or not it was a bluff, we didn't want that kind of friction. We thought about subletting Gomez and Juanita's restaurant, but the space was so full of piñatas that we didn't think we could ever put our own stamp on it.

ANTHONY: So we went door to door on Mission Street, talking with restaurant owners. On the face of it, Lung Shan wasn't an obvious fit, because we'd been looking for a place more conducive to counter service. There was no counter there; it was also a remarkably unpopular and pretty run-down Chinese restaurant in a Hispanic neighborhood. But of all the restaurants we propositioned, Lung Shan was the only one interested.

Surprisingly, the whole negotiation with the owners, Sue and Liang, lasted about one minute. I proposed subletting their kitchen and dining room every Thursday for $300. They countered with $400 and the right to continue their own delivery business. We agreed to start at $300 and try a shared kitchen arrangement.

KAREN: During this bargaining session, I hid out on the sidewalk because I don't speak Cantonese and didn't want to be a complicating (read: white) factor. Having missed the initial conversation, I was murky on the details but intrigued to learn that the owners had also offered to sell the restaurant outright. (This offer is still reiterated every few days). At first, Anthony thought the price was $22,000 for the whole restaurant, and we seriously discussed taking out a loan if things went well. Later, this turned out to be the first of many Cantonese miscommunications: Liang had offered the place for "twenty-two $10,000s."

In the end, I'm glad we didn't buy Lung Shan. Had we just opened our own little restaurant in our own little space, we probably wouldn't be writing this book.

After talking to Lung Shan, we continued our search out of due diligence. I took the lead when we spoke with Latino businesses, because I spoke Spanish. We had a follow-up conversation with the owner of a spot just two doors down from Lung Shan called El Herradero, but that was our only other lead. We were determined to stay on Mission Street in order to keep our name and maintain the improbable momentum we'd established with the truck. A few days later, we blogged about changing from "Mission Street-Food" to "Mission-Street Food" and started thinking about how to pull off a full-scale restaurant—or rather, a restaurant within another restaurant.

Mission Street Food

presents

THE VANGUARD CHRONICLE

THREE WEEKS AGO, ANTHONY MYINT AND HIS WIFE KAREN LEIBOWITZ STARTED A PROJECT CALLED MISSION STREET FOOD.

EACH WEEK THEY SUBLET A GUATEMALAN TACO TRUCK AND SERVED THEIR OWN REENGINEERED "TACOS"— BUTTERY FLATBREADS STUFFED WITH HIGH-QUALITY FILLINGS.

(THIS WAS BEFORE EVERYONE WAS ENAMORED WITH FOOD TRUCKS...

MISSION

...AND BOUTIQUE CUPCAKE VENDORS...

Antojitos San Miguel

...AND TRAVELING SOUFFLÉ CARTS.)

MSF WAS A HIT. THEY'D BEATEN BACK SWELLING MASSES OF FOODIES EACH WEEK WITH FLATBREADS AND *PORK BELLY*.

KAREN AND ANTHONY BOTH HAD FULL-TIME JOBS. IT'S NOT LIKE THEY NEEDED *MORE* WORK.

BUT NEITHER OF THEM COULD EVER SAY NO TO A GOOD IDEA.

FOODIES ARE A PARTICULARLY **DEVOUT** BREED — WILLING TO ENDURE INTERMINABLE LINES AND INCLEMENT WEATHER FOR **A TASTE.**

SAN FRANCISCANS ARE NO EXCEPTION.

BY THIS FOURTH NIGHT OF MISSION STREET FOOD, THE GOSPEL HAD FULLY DISSEMINATED, AND A LINE HAD FORMED EARLIER THAN USUAL.

MSF HAD SOLD OUT OF FOOD EVERY WEEK. ANTHONY WAS DETERMINED NOT TO DISAPPOINT **ANYONE** TONIGHT.

BUT THERE WERE OTHER FORCES AT WORK.

THIS FRIDGE IS SUCH A PIECE OF...

OKAY. I WON'T *SMILE*, BUT I STILL DON'T KNOW WHO YOU *ARE*.

THIS WHOLE OPERATION IS *ILLEGAL*. YOU ARE BREAKING A *FUCKING PROMISE*. HOW MANY TIMES ARE WE GOING TO HAVE THIS CONVERSATION?!?

WE'VE ONLY BEEN HERE FOR THREE WEEKS. WE'VE NEVER TALKED.

I'M *NOT* LEAVING HERE UNTIL THIS IS SHUT DOWN!

J.J. HAD HAD PREVIOUS RUN-INS WITH THE *MIDDLE-AGED GUATEMALAN COUPLE* THAT OWNED THE TACO TRUCK.

AND WHILE KAREN AND ANTHONY WERE ALSO A COUPLE RUNNING THE TACO TRUCK...

Antojitos San Miguel

...THEY DIDN'T EXACTLY LOOK GUATEMALAN.

OR MIDDLE-AGED.

OR LIKE THEY KNEW WHAT HE'S TALKING ABOUT.

YOU GUYS ARE BARKING UP THE WRONG *FUCKING* TREE.

AND YOU'RE GOING TO GET A BILL FROM MY ACCOUNTING DEPARTMENT FOR STEAM-CLEANING THE SIDEWALK.

I'M CALLING THE *POLICE*.

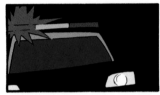

HEY BUDDY, YOU MIND IF I LOOK AT YOUR SELLER'S PERMIT?

IT'S ALL RIGHT. I JUST NEED TO SEE THAT *SOMEONE'S* ALLOWED TO BE HERE.

YEAH. WE ACTUALLY SUBLET THIS TRUCK FROM SOMEONE ELSE. IT'S THEIR PERMIT.

YOU CAN'T DRINK OUTSIDE. I DON'T CARE IF IT'S IN A *PAPER BAG.*

DITCH THAT SHIT, DUDE.

DID THAT ASSHOLE CALL THE *COPS?*

THIS LOOKS FINE. YOU GUYS HAVE TO MAKE SURE YOU CLEAN UP, BUT I DON'T KNOW, THIS SEEMS FINE.

THANKS...

...THAT GUY JUST HAD AN ADULT HISSY-FIT.

MR. VANGUARD LOOKED INTO IT, AND YOUR PERMIT IS FOR SELLING *FRUIT* AND *ICE CREAM ONLY.* IF YOU TRY TO SELL *COOKED* FOOD AGAIN FROM THAT TRUCK, THE POLICE WILL BE BACK TO SHUT YOU DOWN.

HE DIDN'T BELIEVE US WHEN WE TOLD HIM THAT LAST NIGHT WOULD BE OUR LAST.

DO YOU THINK IT'S A BLUFF?

BUT I HATE THE IDEA OF HIM THINKING HE *WON.*

I DON'T WANT TO GET GOMEZ IN TROUBLE. I NEED TO TALK WITH HIM.

WHEN GOMEZ AND JUANITA—THE COUPLE WHO OWNED THE TACO TRUCK—FOUND OUT WHAT HAPPENED, THEY OFFERED TO SUBLET THEIR RESTAURANT SPACE TO ANTHONY.

BUT THEIR RESTAURANT WAS LOCATED IN AN OUT-OF-THE-WAY CORNER OF THE MISSION DISTRICT.

AND WHILE MSF'S CUSTOMERS HAD SHOWN A *QUICK* LOYALTY...

...HOW *FAR* CAN YOU EXPECT PEOPLE TO FOLLOW YOU?

ANTHONY AND KAREN WENT DOOR TO DOOR LOOKING FOR A PLACE THAT WOULD HOST MSF ON A WEEKLY BASIS, PREFERABLY ON MISSION STREET, SO THEY COULD KEEP THEIR NAME.

I SHOULD HAVE PRACTICED MY SPANISH. THIS IS IMPOSSIBLE TO EXPLAIN.

THE OWNER ISN'T HERE. YOU CAN'T HAVE HER NUMBER. WHY SHOULD WE *TRUST* YOU?

THIS PLACE IS CLOSED ON THURSDAYS AND *EVERYTHING!*

WHERE'S EVERYBODY'S ENTREPRENEURIAL *SPIRIT?*

THERE WASN'T MUCH REASON TO BELIEVE THAT A RESTAURANT INSIDE *ANOTHER* RESTAURANT WOULD WORK.

BUT THERE WAS SOMETHING RIDICULOUSLY FUNNY ABOUT SERVING *UPSCALE* FOOD IN A *RUN-DOWN* JOINT...

AND NEITHER OF THEM COULD EVER SAY NO TO A *BAD IDEA.*

LUNG SHAN RES...

LET'S TRY THIS PLACE.

PART TWO

THE RESTAURANT

Life lesson:
A decrepit Chinese joint with
a reputation for long waits
and communal seating doesn't
really scream romance.

ANTHONY: The days were so full back then, and things changed so quickly that my perception of MSF still hadn't shifted from hobby to potential new career—we were just focused on making it through each week. Moving from the truck to the restaurant meant a lot less uncertainty in the hours leading up to service, but it also posed some daunting questions: how would we provide table service? What kind of menu would we offer? What would the ambiance be like? I suppose these are the questions facing most restaurateurs, and at least we weren't faced with a mountain of debt. We did, however, have the added handicap of Lung Shan's crummy flatware and swampy bathroom. We hoped to just attribute any false notes to cultural differences. The grubby carpet wouldn't reflect on us, right?

KAREN: Some of our friends helped with the décor, which amounted to turning off the hospital-style fluorescent lights and putting up Christmas lights. Fortunately, Lung Shan already had an amazing collection of surreal large-format posters from China—Communist leaders on horseback, soaring phoenixes, and such (*see picture on next page*). We decided to try conventional table service, with a contingency plan calling for a shift to dim-sum-style service if we got overwhelmed. We wanted to open for dinner at 6:00, but I couldn't get back from teaching in Berkeley until 7:00, so our friends would help out until then. The planning meeting was brief, and it mostly revolved around writing cheeky fortunes to stuff inside Anthony's sesame cookies, which would accompany the check. We were deluding ourselves.

Bear in mind that neither Anthony nor I had ever waited tables before. I'd worked behind the counter at a café for a few years in college, but I didn't know much about the rhythms of table service. And we really hadn't thought through the implications of moving to Lung Shan, which appeared to be a functional restaurant but never had more than a dozen eat-in customers at once. We told ourselves that we'd be a little busier than they were, but not much, at least not at first. We truly believed that the novelty of the truck had been the main draw to MSF.

We only skipped one Thursday between our last night in the truck and our first night in the restaurant, which accounts for some of our disorganization, but even with more time, we couldn't have anticipated certain problems. Of course, we knew in an abstract sense that customers in a sit-down restaurant expect that water will be brought to them, but we didn't realize what that would mean at Lung Shan, where the lone water pitcher was refilled at the kitchen's only faucet, interrupting whoever was washing dishes.

There's no such thing as a
lesbian dragonfly.

A two-story-tall wolf is scarier
than a Tyrannosaurus Rex.

Man is the only animal that flies
airplanes.

Mounds of organic trash are
piled up on your naked,
supine body, my friend.

**FORTUNE COOKIES AND
COMMUNIST PROPAGANDA**

*(Previous page) The A/V corner of the
Lung Shan dining room.*

*(Above) Fortunes that were tucked
inside sesame tuile cookies on the first
night at Lung Shan.*

(Next page) The Lung Shan floorplan.

Every single process had a glitch like that. Perhaps we should have considered a soft opening. Things were so foreign (and we were so clueless) that it felt like we were anthropologists piecing together the idea of a restaurant from pictographs and shards of pottery.

ANTHONY: Leading up to the start of our first dinner service, I started to feel the pressure of single-handedly prepping out a whole restaurant, exacerbated by the judgmental gaze of the *shifu* (the Chinese chef with whom we shared the hot line). On the bright side, we had a full-size deep fryer, four burners, and an oven at our disposal. We also had a wok, with which I planned to make fried rice. In a corny twist, we called it "MSF rice," which ostensibly stood for "meated, smoked, and fried" (*see page 168*). Another dish we served was one of my favorite dishes from childhood, *ohno kauswe*—a traditional coconut curry and chicken noodle soup with lots of garnishes. We served it at our wedding, and it's a crowd-pleaser.

Chris Ying was helping me cook, but despite our respective years in the restaurant industry, we were not prepared. As soon as we opened, orders started coming in five or six at a time, but the metal ticket holder was broken. We were stacking tickets on the only available surface in the kitchen, which was the narrow counter where we were also plating food. Tickets were sticking to dishes, or getting greasy and illegible. When duplicate tickets started showing up, disorganization turned to utter chaos. Finally, we decided to completely disregard tickets and just make random batches of each dish as fast as we could. I can only imagine

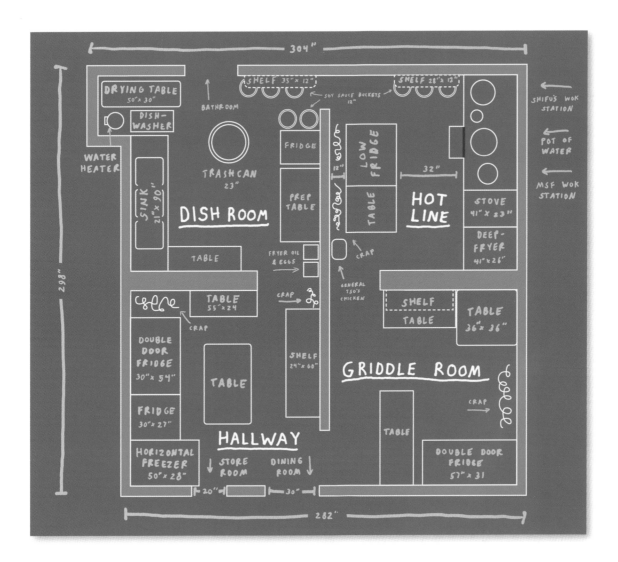

what the dining room must have been like, because I never even left the kitchen.

KAREN: My memories of that night are hazy. As I sprinted the two blocks from the BART station, I saw a crowd standing outside the restaurant and wondered if they'd had to evacuate for some reason. I ran faster. As I opened the door, I saw a completely full house, and it seemed like everyone I knew

was there. Half a dozen of our friends had spontaneously stepped in to help. My old roommate Simon was walking around with a bunch of open beers and our friend Carlo Espinas[5] had become our official bathroom-traffic director ("All the way at the back. Thank you!"). It was unclear who was a

---

5 Carlo is the chef of Comstock Saloon and an all-around good guy.

INSIDE LUNG SHAN

A Chinese restaurant's kitchen is unlike any other.
(Clockwise from top left) The pantry/storage hallway/restaurant owner's
sleeping den; Lung Shan's "sitting room," a.k.a. MSF's garde manger station;
available counter space + electric griddle + butane burner + rice cooker = cooking station;
the hot line, where MSF and Lung Shan shared space.

server and who was a customer, and even people I didn't know seemed familiar, like in a dream, though I probably recognized some of them from the truck. (Then again, a lot of people in the Mission look the same to me, particularly now that beards have come back into fashion.)

The new MSF had been open for about an hour, and it was an utter shit show. They had switched over to dim-sum-style service, and the tables closest to the kitchen were gobbling up all the food, leaving the tables farther away from the kitchen hungry and pissy. The beer was warm. The cash register was broken, so a friend was doing all the check calculations with pencil and paper in the dark.

As a group, we had no system, no table numbers, no common language for the food we were serving. We were laughably inept. No one wanted to wash dishes full-time, so we took turns randomly going to the back to clean whatever we were desperate for. At the end of the night, I worked that dishwasher for what seemed like hours, wondering how I had arrived at this point in my life. I could hear Anthony talking with the owners of Lung Shan behind me in Cantonese, but I couldn't understand a word. I thought, "They'd better be talking about what a good wife I am."

When we got home, I felt exhausted to the point of despondency, but I also felt a little bit sentimental. Anthony had become a chef. I had become a restaurant manager/dishwasher. Our friends were pulling for us. We were incompetent. We were successful. Nothing made any sense. I felt really lucky.

THE FIRST NIGHT IN LUNG SHAN

*(Clockwise from top left) One of the first items on the MSF menu—
ohno kauswe, a Burmese coconut curry soup; Anthony garnishing soups
after the switch to dim-sum–style service; the watchful gaze of shifu.*

GUEST CHEFS

Over the twenty-month run of MSF, seventy guest chefs passed through our kitchen (pictured below are Jordan Grosser and Tia Harrison). Initially, we found them by way of this questionnaire:

If you are interested in being a guest chef at Mission Street Food, please email us with the information below at *missionstreetfood@gmail.com*.

As a guest chef, you should buy your own ingredients and prep 3–4 dishes on your own, with some exceptions (both as to the number of dishes and the amount of help we can provide). Same-day prep can be done at our kitchen, but as much prep as possible should be done in advance and presumably in a commercial kitchen. Money earned from your dish will be yours to keep, less 20 percent for shared costs. For example, if you sell 50 orders of a $10 dish, you will receive $400 to cover your time and food costs and we will use the other $100 to pay for overhead. We will staff the front of the house and will also have one or more cooks available if you need help serving your dishes. We will donate our profits to charity and you can decide whether or not to donate a portion of your proceeds to a charity of your choosing.

Creativity is encouraged, and our typical menu items are substantive small plates. Please refer to our blog for an example of past menu items and prices. Also bear in mind that the kitchen will be shared and that space and time are often limited, so your dishes should have a fairly quick and/or easy pick-up. The kitchen has four small burners, three deep-fryer baskets, a wok, another pot of boiling water on a wok burner, and a small oven (can fit a 6" hotel pan or half sheet).

NAME:
PHONE:
EMAIL:
PREFERRED DATES (THURSDAYS):
COOKING EXPERIENCE (BRIEFLY):
PROPOSED DISHES:
QUESTIONS/COMMENTS:

ANTHONY: In spite of our inefficiency, we still managed to serve much more food from the restaurant than we ever did from the truck. That meant more prep, more storage, and more imposition on Bar Tartine. By mid-November, MSF's welcome in Jason's kitchen was wearing thin. I was at a decision point, and even though the future was entirely uncertain, I gave notice at Bar Tartine and agreed to a part-time schedule until they found my replacement. It wasn't much of a personal risk, since I'd only been making about $12 an hour.

KAREN: Anthony also had the idea to invite cooks from around the city to join us as guest chefs. These visitors could not only share the burden of prep, but also broaden our customer base by bringing their friends. When he pitched the idea to me, I said the first thing that came to my mind, which was "You are a radical thinker!" Seriously. Looking back, I think that was truer than I realized at the time. Anthony does things differently from other people; he sees possibilities where no one else does, but he's also willing to take on projects that everyone else is too practical to even try.

ANTHONY: After two MSF-only menus, we took off for three weeks around Thanksgiving to regroup, stall while Bar Tartine hired my replacement, and sit back and wait for guest-chef proposals to come pouring in—with so many talented line

cooks in the Bay Area, we thought we'd be launching a whole indie-chef movement.

Over those three weeks, several new hires flaked out on Bar Tartine, and there was no flood of guest-chef applications, but Chris put us in touch with one prospect.

KAREN: Tia Harrison ran an artisanal butcher shop and was the chef of Sociale, an upscale Italian restaurant. We met her for a planning meeting in a secret party room in the back of her butcher shop. That was disconcerting enough, but Tia kept confounding us with completely reasonable questions for which we had no reasonable answers:

> *How much food?*
> We don't know exactly.
> *How many cooks?*
> It depends.
> *How will the money work?*
> You'll pay for everything and then later we'll give you a bunch of cash. Trust us.

ANTHONY: The system we devised involved splitting the menu roughly evenly, with guest chefs setting their own prices and paying for their own food costs. MSF would collect 20 percent of the guest chef's total sales toward overhead and taxes. Guests got to choose the theme, and we would follow suit. For Tia's guest-chef night, our blog advertised a "Southern-style menu inspired by butter, hip-hop, and gentrification: 'The Dirty

South Cleans Up Pretty Good.'" This was my chance to make a dessert I'd been fantasizing about for a while: butter-fried cornbread with buttermilk panna cotta and candied sage (*see pages 199 and 200*), which turned into an "MSF classic" that I'd return to many times.

KAREN: Tia brought her own servers, and that certainly helped. We numbered the tables and each server took five of the fifteen; everything became much more orderly. I took up my place by the cash register, which became my command post for most of the next year.

MSF picked up momentum with our next guest chef, Ryan Farr, who was on his way to becoming a "celebrity butcher" (though that label disguises the fact that he's the nicest guy ever). Ryan brought his own servers, too: his lovely wife Cesalee, a very drunk waiter, and another guy named Adam who became a regular MSF server/resident smart-ass.

ANTHONY: Ryan would make two guest-chef appearances. The first one's theme was pork, so he brought his unbelievably light homemade *chicharrones*, a ham-and-pork terrine, a homemade pork-and-kumquat sausage, and a bacon-and-apple cookie. Among other things, we offered our own porky dessert: pecan pie with lines of bacon "snow" served on mirrors. This involved a technique that Jason used at Bar Tartine to transform fats into powders. The "snow"

was reasonably tasty, but more importantly, it fueled the flames of publicity. For a few days, local food blogs were abuzz with MSF's bacon snow, wondering whether it was meant to be snorted (*see page 86*).

By the third week of the new format, we were already scrambling to find guest chefs. This would prove to be an issue for the duration of Mission Street Food. Since there were barely any guest-chef proposals, especially at first, we often resorted to pressuring our cook-friends to step up to the plate. The final MSF of 2008 was a hodgepodge of people we already knew, each contributing a single dish to a "Mash-Up Night" that deliberately mixed regional cuisines. We played a soundtrack of mash-ups and generally had a good time. Once again, food journalists and bloggers jumped on the story.

KAREN: Over the holidays, Anthony and I visited a new ice cream shop in the Mission at the end of its first day. Humphry Slocombe was deserted that evening—it's not easy opening an ice cream shop in December—though it's been packed ever since. That night, we tried all of their flavors, which tend

GUEST CHEF DISHES

(*Top*) *Ted Fleury and Jordan Grosser's duck heart and foie gras on a stick, with royal trumpet mushrooms, creamy polenta, and cherry.*

(*Bottom*) *Chad Newton's composition of cooked, raw, marinated, and pickled vegetables, with wheat berries, meyer lemon aioli, and dark rye crumbs.*

FATTY McFATFAT

For a while, Mission Street Food's popularity was grotesquely out of proportion with its capacity. People would line up for an hour or more before the doors opened, and they might wait more than two hours for a table. At 6 p.m., diners would stream in, fill all the seats, and order everything on the menu. We were bursting at the seams, spilling customers onto the sidewalk, while those inside stuffed every last morsel into their mouths. It was exhilarating. It was disgusting.

MSF ran out of food almost every night, and we scrambled to replace one decadent ingredient with another. No more pork belly? Bring on the duck confit we were saving for Saturday. No more buttery flatbreads? Slide that duck confit onto some chips with some goat cheese, and make nachos. As the night would wind down, we'd cover the menu with substitutions, and people kept ordering until the new dishes ran out, too. It hardly seemed to matter what we served, as long as it delivered a little novelty and plenty of richness. (*See "The Sportification of Food," page 78.*)

As purveyors of "street food," we promised exotic treats to which the usual dietary laws would not apply. These were just small plates—little tastes of unrelenting variety that encouraged sampling and tapped into unconscious triggers for overeating. Science has now confirmed what you no doubt already know through experience: "Variety Enhances Food Intake in Humans,"[1] "Tasting Different Foods Delays Satiation,"[2] and "Increased variety in the food supply may contribute to the development and maintenance of obesity."[3] Each dish seems like a fun indulgence until they add up to a 3,000-calorie meal.

It surely didn't help that most people shared dishes with their friends, since this scrambles the visual cues that are central to gauging fullness. A study of hunger and satisfaction at the University of Illinois showed that eaters of all shapes and sizes

DINNER FOR TWO, FOR ONE

An MSF dish, comprising a meatball sandwich with Gruyère fonduta, AND a biscuit with sausage-loaded gravy.

ate 73 percent more soup from rigged "self-refilling" bowls than they did from regular bowls; furthermore, these eaters "did not believe that they had consumed more, nor did they perceive themselves as more sated than those eating from normal bowls."[4] At MSF and most small-plates restaurants, dishes come out one or two at a time, and plates are cleared away to make room for the next course—another self-refilling soup bowl of sorts.

So if we contributed to the chronically diseased America you see today, we apologize. We were young, idealistic, and hungry, and if it's any consolation, we gained weight, too.

---

1 L. Brond*el, et al.* "Variety Enhances Food Intake in Humans; role of sensory specific satiety." *Physiol Behav* 97 (2009): 44-51.

2 M.M. Hetherington, *et al.* "Understanding Variety: Tasting Different Foods Delays Satiation." *Physiol Behav* 87 (2006): 263–271.

3 H. A. Raynor, *et al.* "Dietary Variety, Energy Regulation, and Obesity." *Psychol Bulletin* 127 (2001): 325–341.

4 Brian Wansink, *et al.* "Bottomless Bowls: Why Visual Cues of Portion Size May Influence Intake." *Obesity Research* 13 (2005): 93–100.

to be pretty inventive, and bought a scoop of "Secret Breakfast" (bourbon ice cream with corn-flake crunchies). We thought that MSF and Humphry Slocombe would be a good fit, so we talked to one of the owners, Jake Godby, who looked bemused when we tried to explain our business model. He's hilariously soft-spoken, but he seemed glad to have his first restaurant account.

It became part of my Thursday routine to stop by Humphry Slocombe to pick up a couple gallons of whatever flavor we were serving and chat with Jake and his co-owner, Sean Vahey. These days, they're famous, with their 300,000 Twitter followers, book deal, and TV appearances, but back then, we were just two improbable start-up businesses helping each other out. We take it for granted now that there's an amazing ice cream shop a few blocks away, but when I pull back and get some perspective, I have to admit: Jake is a genius of ice cream, Sean is a genius of publicity, and we were lucky to meet those guys when we did.

ANTHONY: As we moved into 2009, we committed to Mission Street Food by having Lung Shan hire me as a part-time chef and Mission Street Food as food consultants. MSF acquired a business license, tax ID number, worker's comp insurance, and its first employee. As sous chef/flatbread machine, Emma Sullivan stuck with us for an entire year. I first met Emma at Bar Tartine, but we worked together much more closely at MSF, where her dedication, common sense, and baking skills were invaluable. She worked some of our busiest nights, when there were waits of over two hours, but also some of our least glamorous nights, when it was just the two of us in the kitchen trying to make ends meet.

Around the same time, we introduced the charitable component to our already complicated business model. Our blog made it sound like a brand-new idea, but in fact, it was a fulfillment of the benevolent business plan that I'd conceived long before Mission Street Food. When MSF took off, I thought, Why not start now? The idea of a benevolent food business was an extension of what I'd seen my dad doing all those years—giving fruit to homeless people and migrant workers—combined with my own enthusiasm for artery-clogging delicacies, which he didn't really share. In fact, he swore off all pork when he was a young man, based on a fortuneteller's advice, and he expected the same porcine abstinence from his children.

KAREN: Anthony and I had discussed his plans for a charitable business before we got married, and I was on board (though I also hoped we'd bring in more than the graduate-student wages I was making at that point—$15,000 per year is not a lot to live on in the Bay Area.) Then again, January 2009 was a hopeful and auspicious time. Obama was about to be inaugurated, and people were saying "Yes We Can!" with

real earnestness. Anthony and I decided to donate all of our profits to local hunger-related charities, drawing just a limited salary for ourselves. We live in a studio apartment, and we're pretty frugal (except for occasional splurges at nice restaurants). Anthony really believes in benevolent business, and I support him in that.

ANTHONY: It's not like I'm a selfless good Samaritan. On a personal level, I feel like the charitable commitment eases my conscience about moral shortcomings, like eating meat in spite of its carbon footprint. From a marketing perspective, it gave us access to the grassroots networks of our beneficiaries, extending our reach beyond hipsters and foodies. And in terms of

SAN FRANCISCO FOOD CHARITIES

(Above) The San Francisco Food Bank.
(Page 64–65) The Food Pantry at St. Gregory's.

publicity, being charitable drew even more press coverage to MSF than we'd had as *merely* an occasional restaurant-within-a-restaurant featuring nightly guest-chefs. That said, I felt pretty great walking out of Project Open Hand[6] after making that first donation. I didn't even have to yell at anyone about bananas, hopefully sidestepping my genetic predisposition toward charity-induced hypertension.

---

6 Project Open Hand delivers groceries and meals to home-bound seniors and people with HIV/AIDS in San Francisco.

BENEVOLENT BUSINESS

Early on at Mission Street Food, we decided to roll out a business model we'd been dreaming of for a long time. Each night we donated all of our net profits to local charities. After that, we opened three other restaurants under the same benevolent business rubric, but with donations in proportion to what they sell (e.g. $1 from each Mission Burger sale went to the SF Food Bank).

Our advocacy of benevolent business is based on our assumption that the benefits of donating money (publicity, brand loyalty, promotional assistance from beneficiaries) outweigh the costs (literally giving money away). But the honest truth is that we have no idea whether a charitable component is actually "good for business." We've argued about its effectiveness with each other, with our families, and with our friends, to no avail. But we persist in giving money away, because, while it's unprovable, the logic seems pretty sound to us.

First and foremost is the assertion that a charitable agenda drives business. Today there are countless products with a socially responsible component, ranging from fair-trade coffee, to the extreme example of TOMS shoes, which donates a pair of shoes for each pair they sell. The "ethical" product is theoretically more attractive than its socially neutral counterparts and as such, either demands a premium ($1/lb more for fair-trade coffee) or results in greater demand generally (if they were the same price, more consumers would choose the fair-trade coffee).

Thus the goal of benevolent business is not to simply offer an ethical product, but to imbue any product or service with an ethical association.

Okay, so this isn't news. Most intuitive business owners have identified that this is an option, but the instincts that keep them in business scream: *not worth it!* We still wonder if it's worth it. We suspect that if we made donations optional, many consumers would simply opt for a lower price (and heck, maybe we would have been just as successful running optionally benevolent businesses). But we also suspect that if Chez Panisse opened a non-local, non-sustainable, non-organic, non–seasonal produce-driven restaurant, it would be a flop. Likewise, twenty years ago, business owners probably would have had little interest in switching from cheap styrofoam packaging to expensive, drastically inferior packaging made from postconsumer material.

So even though it's hard to quantify, we think there's a demonstrable increase in demand for ethical products over their socially neutral counterparts. And theoretically, if pledging to donate to charity nets you $1,000 more in sales, with a 10 percent profit margin, you could then give as much as $100 to charity.

In addition to direct financial benefits, the benevolent business model opens potential doors for cross-promotion—marketing conducted by the beneficiary. A good example of that might be, say, how a portion of the proceeds from this book benefit Slow Food USA, and in turn, they've agreed to help us sell the crap out of it.

Finally, there are the intrinsic benefits. From a consumer perspective, there may be an associated increase in satisfaction, like an unavoidable transference of ethical approval onto the actual experience. ("I can taste how much I'm helping farmers with each sip of this fair-trade coffee.") There are undeniable intrinsic benefits from a business owner's perspective, too: a sense of accomplishment, improved employee job satisfaction (which can result in improved work ethic and retention rate). And in the long run, even if donating doesn't significantly improve your bottom line, you're investing in your brand's worth.

In a competitive marketplace full of artisanal chocolatiers and ramenistas, all clawing to be "the best," adding an ethical component can be a distinguishing factor. At MSF we used our charitable agenda to firmly establish ourselves as "the best restaurant within a restaurant, with rotating guest chefs, that also donates to charity."

KAREN: In the coming weeks and months, we visited a bunch of hunger-related charities to see where our donations were going. It was incredible to see the dramatically different scales of each operation, and how there was a distinct culture at each place. The San Francisco Food Bank's corporate headquarters adjoin the massive warehouse from which they deliver millions of pounds of food to pantries across the city. Meanwhile, the St. Anthony Foundation serves 2,600 meals a day, and feels like a cross between a rock concert and a high-school cafeteria during the lunch rush.

ANTHONY: We were also inspired by the small food pantries at the other end of the spectrum, like Martin de Porres, a free restaurant for homeless people. Their dining room is full of art and music, emanating the vibe of a pacifist retirement commune. The men who run Martin de Porres are former Catholic priests who have broken away from the church hierarchy but maintain their vows of poverty; they are fully committed to their work and yet extremely low-key about it, just eating alongside the people they serve and living in a dormitory nearby.

But probably our strongest bond was with The Food Pantry at St. Gregory's in Potrero Hill, whose director even made a guest-chef appearance at MSF. (*See page 68.*)

KAREN: I think that the charitable aspect of MSF also bought us some leniency from the public while we were still working out the kinks. Maybe a spirit of generosity pervaded the place, or maybe it just seemed churlish to gripe about a fundraiser—but in either case, we were given the benefit of the doubt, and we appreciated it.

As the weeks went on, we gradually developed a cadre of regular servers, some of whom had worked with Anthony at Bar Tartine, and others who had come to MSF as customers. It was always amazing to see how they could absorb information about each new menu in a matter of minutes and then describe it with precision and grace for the rest of the night, only to start fresh again the next week.

At the same time, we were also meeting a lot of cooks. The guys at Humphry Slocombe introduced us to Jeff Banker, who was an early guest chef and went on to open the restaurant Baker and Banker with his wife, Lori Baker. Our friend Carlo knows everyone, which helped expand our network of San Francisco cook-friends, and often one guest chef would lead to another. This was the case with Chris Kronner, a celebrated local chef, who brought along a cook known as "Korean Danny."

ANTHONY: We had Kronner scheduled for February 14th. It would be our second Saturday service, cementing the twice-weekly schedule we would maintain for the rest of our time at MSF. Every chef knows that Valentine's Day is the busiest night of the year, but it turned out to be our slow-est night ever. So that was a life lesson: a decrepit Chinese joint with a reputation for long waits and communal seating doesn't really scream romance. Back in the kitchen, though, there was a burgeoning bro-mance. I think Danny admired our divey/refined set-up, and I admired his gourmet/vaga-bond style—here was the reigning world champion of pesto,[7] with his Japanese UX-10 knives Saran-wrapped to a sheet tray for the bike ride home.

KAREN: Normally, our relations with the guest chefs were pretty good, because we all felt like we were going through the wringer together. We'd be shaking hands for the first time in the afternoon and sharing beers by the end of the night. It's important for us to acknowledge how chal-lenging MSF was for the guest chefs—they were asked to pump out a high volume of food from a cruddy kitchen to a throng of would-be food critics, all while adjusting to our systems (and our personalities). There was no real vetting process, and not much meddling with guest-chef menus because we were in no position to criticize or ques-tion anyone's methods. Usually it worked, but not always.

If we did meddle, it was usually too

late. I had to pull the plug on one guest chef who was in over his head. He'd done some catering, but he'd never cooked in a restaurant. It seemed like he didn't even know that his food was bad, but I could see that bowls of his bison stew were coming back uneaten, and then a customer/friend beckoned me over to taste it for myself. That stew was inedible. It tasted like an ashtray made of squirrel meat. I marched into the kitchen and told him he couldn't serve any more of it. That was the one and only time that I eighty-sixed a guest chef's dish.

ANTHONY: In retrospect, we were bound to hit a dud sooner or later. The warning signs were all there, too. When that guest chef arrived at about 1 p.m. that afternoon, I already knew it was time to shift from regular prep to damage control when he was trying to find ice for his bison meat. You'd think his bison stew would be completely ready before he arrived, since stewed meat benefits from slow cooking and an overnight cooling, but in fact, the meat was still a fro-zen block. That was unfortunate, but the real head-scratcher was the ice. This dude wasn't scrambling to thaw the meat, he was worried that it would spoil. At 4 p.m., he rushed the bison meat from his cooler of ice onto the wok burner and—of course—he scorched it.

KAREN: It's incredibly hard on the front-of-house staff to spend the night apologizing to strangers. In the end, I guess I felt bad for the

---

[7] In the summer of 2008, Danny attended the World Pesto Championship in Genoa, Italy. He'd planned to assist the chef of the Italian restaurant where he was working, but when the chef was too hungover to compete, Danny stepped in and won the title himself.

SARA MILES AND THE FOOD PANTRY

by Karen Leibowitz

Sara Miles is the director of The Food Pantry at St. Gregory's. She only cooked at Mission Street Food for one night, but she embodies the best parts of the whole endeavor. She is a practical, hardworking idealist with a sense of humor, and she believes that food is really, really important. She summed up her life story better than we can in her initial guest-chef proposal:

SARA MILES AND PAUL FROMBERG AT ST. GREGORY'S

> *I'm a former restaurant cook and war correspondent. I worked as a journalist for years, then ate a piece of bread and found God. I now feed 750+ a week in Potrero Hill where we cook a 4-course family meal for 40+ volunteers (mostly immigrants, the insane, and the very poor) every week. I preach and cook at St. Gregory of Nyssa Church with my sous (and the priest) Paul [Fromberg]. I've lived in the Mission for 15 years, and work there with gleaners and the free farmstand to feed people.*
>
> *My wife and I raise chickens, apricots, figs, apples, lemons and plums in our Shotwell Street backyard, along with flowers. I'd love to cook you a neighborhood meal (weed tart from Bernal Hill; honey from Capp Street; etc.) with the crucial addition of swine (I regularly make, with Father Paul, our own bacon).*
>
> *I know how to deal with weird kitchens; I have my own knives; I can do a demiglace and a creme anglaise without looking up recipes, and I can handle the public.*
>
> *Let me know—*
> *Sara*

This message arrived in January, within a week of our announcement that we would begin donating our profits, but Sara and Paul didn't actually come to MSF until March. In the intervening time, we visited The Food Pantry, the organization that Sara had founded.

It was amazing. Every Friday, St. Gregory of Nyssa Episcopal Church transforms itself into a benevolent farmers market, where fresh produce and other healthy foods bring people together under a mural of "dancing saints," from Mohatma Gandhi to Jesus to Ella Fitzgerald, circling the space in a neo-Byzantine ecstasy of goodwill. The altar becomes the centerpiece of the pantry. There are no religious sermons or requirements, but a spiritual resoluteness pervades the place.

Sara started The Food Pantry in 2000 without much experience and without waiting for institutional approval or support. This ethos—of plunging in and trying to fill a need—extends to the larger structure of The Food Pantry, which is operated by a ragtag group of volunteers who, in Sara's words, "came for the food and stayed for the community."

Like MSF, The Food Pantry started out as a weekly event that grew beyond its initial host environment. Sadly, the economic collapse created a seemingly insatiable demand for their services. In the year following Sara's initial email, The Food Pantry expanded from 750 to 1,200 clients, and then could expand no further. Sara and her compatriots have helped other pantries organize around the city, and they continue to do so. We encourage you to get involved.[1]

But back to Sara.

Sara is the kind of Christian you imagine if you read the Gospels and extrapolate from there: she takes Jesus at his word when he tells his followers to love their neighbors and feed the poor. The Food Pantry, in her view, is an extension of Communion, which connects people to each other and to God through the sharing of bread. Her commonsensical practice of Christianity quietly exposes the hypocrisy of religious rhetoric that isn't backed by action. In person, Sara is very warm and excitable; it feels good to talk with her. She nods empathetically as she listens, but she also swears a lot, so she doesn't seem like a pushover.

Early on, Sara saw Mission Street Food as a spiritual endeavor, though she respected our secular orientation. A few days before her stint as a guest chef, she called to ask if she and Paul, the priest at St. Gregory's, could offer Communion at the end of the night. Honestly, this seemed weird. Communion among all the sticky tables, under the Maoist posters, with the noise of the dishwasher in the background? No problem, she told us; "I've done Ash Wednesday services in BART stations!" This was not necessarily reassuring, but we agreed to the idea, perhaps more from a liberal fear of judging others than from anything else.

Sara and Paul wisecracked their way through their afternoon of prep at MSF. The button on Paul's apron said it all: *WTFWJD?* They were the sassy gay 'n' Christian cooking comedy duo! But for all their can-do spirit, they seemed a bit overwhelmed when the orders started rolling in. The place was packed from six to ten, and they were hustling the entire time.

When it was all over, they invited everyone— cooks, servers, dishwasher, and the last few diners— to gather around for Communion. We stood together, tired and sweaty, and passed some baguette and a glass of wine while we said a short prayer. Nothing momentous happened, but it was nice to acknowledge that we had been through something together.

Communion at MSF felt more like a post-game pep-talk than church, but Sara's definition of church is pretty expansive. For her, The Food Pantry is church because it's "hundreds of people gathering around an altar to share food and to thank God." Likewise, Sara thought it was church for MSF to seat strangers together, though frankly we did it because we didn't have enough tables. Couples met (or ignored) each other at four-tops, and groups were forced to mingle at our only big table. In Sara's eyes, our vaguely disreputable practice became a spiritual accomplishment. Suddenly it seemed like we were not just giving to charity, but actually building community.

When Sara wrote about MSF in her book, *Jesus Freak*, she emphasized how restaurants and churches feed the same human need for connection: "I'd thought, when I first started serving in church, how much it reminded me of working in restaurants. But I didn't realize that restaurant people might also be looking for a way to create, in their hot kitchens and crazy rushed services, an experience of communion." She recalls that night at MSF as a moment of grace, but she also admits that Anthony seemed more concerned with the rice and beans we were selling than the bread and wine we shared during our impromptu Communion.

Sara's brand of spiritual optimism resonated with MSF's brand of resourcefulness—we both like to redefine failures as virtues. Her religious orientation celebrates society's outcasts, and in doing so, she recaptures some of the original radical spirit of Christianity. In a mundane way, Mission Street Food threatened some conventional practices, as well. We don't believe in God, but like Sara, we believe that God loves weirdos.

---

1 Visit *thefoodpantry.org* for more information.

A UNIQUE ARRANGEMENT

(Above) Emma Sullivan, MSF's first sous chef.

(Opposite page, top) Over time, the kitchen sharing became almost natural.

(Opposite page, bottom) Sue and Liang team-cook a takeout order.

(Page 72–73) The griddle room and adjacent hallway area, two parts of Lung Shan's quirky multi-room kitchen.

guy, but we learned to be more wary of guest chefs with limited restaurant experience.

ANTHONY: That was in February 2009. It's strange to think of all that happened in those first few months: we started the truck in October, moved into Lung Shan in November, hosted our first guest chef in December, went charitable in January, and opened for two nights a week in February. After we met Danny on Valentine's Day, we convinced him to take my place at Bar Tartine. Once I was able to devote myself to MSF full time, I guess I started to get comfortable with our surroundings. The old cardboard that Lung Shan laid down on the floor to absorb oil spills seemed increasingly rational, and the grime on the walls faded out of my consciousness.

I even had my first stereotypical Chinese-restaurant moment when I threw a cleaver at a mouse. It was a huge fatty, and when I missed, it simply moseyed off with no sense of its impending extinction. I later discovered it under a table in the dining room and asked Sue if I should kill it. She said, "If you can kill it, go ahead and kill it." Not wanting to make a bloody mess, I struck it with the backside of an old, dull cleaver. It shrieked and ran off, and I felt like a complete failure until we discovered its corpse in a corner behind the register. Apparently I had dealt it a fatal blow without even breaking the skin! Was this my proudest MSF moment?

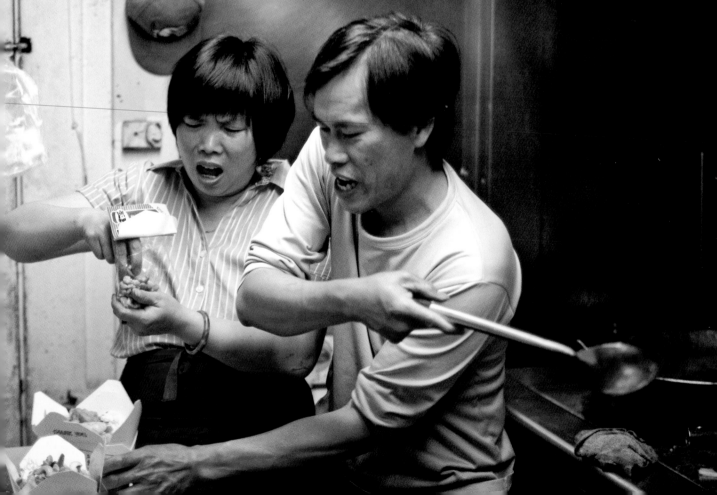

LIFE IN A CHINESE KITCHEN

by Anthony Myint

I always felt like I had a pretty good grasp of the Chinese approach to life—I've spent time in China and in American Chinatowns, and I lived with my Chinese grandmother until I was twenty-five—but nothing prepared me for the thousands of hours I'd spend in an actual Chinese kitchen with actual Chinese cooks. Here are some notes from my cultural immersion.

On Food Safety

Every time you eat chow mein or fried rice, chances are the strips of meat have spent some time being "washed" in a sink, because "slaughterhouses are dirty." Specifically, this means a large case of frozen boneless meat was carved on a deli slicer into $1/4$" slabs and then thawed in a sink with a splash of water and a pinch of baking soda.

I've worked in fine-dining restaurants where cooks scrub down a stainless-steel sink and fill it with water to wash greens. While this is a similar approach, five pounds of greens floating in ten gallons of water seems more reasonable than forty pounds of lightly moistened raw meat crammed in a basin. But by the twentieth sink-full of raw meat, you stop noticing it, just like you stopped noticing the eggs and commercial mayonnaise kept at room temperature.

On Chinese Medicine

Chicken soup is a common remedy in a lot of cultures, and it played a part in my acceptance of Eastern medicine for a brief period. When I had a cold, Liang would offer me some chicken soup with ginger and boiled peanuts—a standard staff lunch among Lung Shan's employees. I would feel better despite (or perhaps due to) the abundance of MSG.

Then one night I accidentally splashed smoking-hot beef fat on my hand during a busy night. At the next lull in service I reached for the burn cream, which happened to be in a cardboard box above Shifu's station. He addressed me like I was an idiot and insisted that I put salt on the already-forming blisters. "If you put salt on it you'll be very comfortable and not have any bubbles," he promised.

In the heat of the moment, I caved to social pressure—hey, MSG chicken soup had done the trick, so it seemed plausible that salt could draw out the moisture from a burn and prevent a blister. I literally poured salt in my wounds, ending up with the worst blisters ever and a scar on my hand as a reminder to be skeptical of Chinese medicine. Cultural immersion has its limits after all.

As weeks and months passed, our days took on a sort of semi-dysfunctional family feeling. Sue would spend hours every day napping in her easy chair and watching Mandarin-dubbed Korean melodramas. Emma and I would split a burrito at the family table with Sue's mom, whom we called The Old Lady. She speaks no English at all, which is fine because none of us really spoke with anyone from a different generation while we were working. The one exception was Liang, who took breaks from napping in his car to offer to sell me the restaurant before leaving to snake the drains. Liang talks about antiques and women far too often, and in a way I find uncomfortable, but you gotta hand it to the guy. If the restaurant's full and a master fuse blows, he'll save the day by hacking a chunk off of a steel pipe and jamming it in the fuse box.

One of the main reasons Emma put up with Liang and the demanding and unpredictable schedule at MSF was its educational value. When you work with about fifty different chefs in a year, you learn a lot, especially about how the industry works. You see some disheartening stuff, like executive chefs who hand their Mexican prep cooks cans of vegetables and a page from a magazine, then leave for a couple hours. You see people who can barely handle cooking two dishes go on to open their own restaurants, and people who've cooked at three-Michelin-star establishments fade out of the profession. And you see chefs who were told to bring sixty orders proceed to bring two hundred, and fret over the extra orders they're stuck with at the end of the night.

But you also see inspiring stuff. You see highly skilled chefs making the food they really want to eat, and not just Northern Italian "California cuisine." You see chefs walk into the dining room and get a standing ovation. And you see kitchen brigades so organized that their stations are set up an hour early and they're scrubbing down your kitchen and equipment. We learned about exotic delights like *yamamomo* and homegrown delicacies like Colonel Newsom's country ham. We got to see how seasoned professionals handled sweetbreads and sourdough bread, what worked and what didn't work, what we liked and didn't like.

We also learned by doing. Whenever we had a guest chef, we still made ourselves responsible for 30–50 percent of the menu. Since we ceded the hot line to the guest chefs, we were forced to make do with a portable burner, a rice steamer, and an electric griddle set up in the margins of the kitchen. Guest chefs chose the theme, and we responded with ideas of our own. It required considerable flexibility and forced us to be extremely strategic, which is probably my only noteworthy quality as a chef. Working the way we did, it wasn't really a matter of artistry, but rather, optimization of resources. Which usually just meant putting in more hours or more *umami*.

KAREN: We never indicated which dishes came from MSF and which came from the guest chefs, but now that MSF is over, I have to admit that my favorite dishes were Anthony's. Of course, there were many amazing dishes by guest chefs and many misses by our crew, but I doubt MSF would have survived without the baseline of Anthony's dishes. It's all the more impressive given that he had the added constraint of filling in the gaps. If we needed a vegetarian or lower-priced option to balance out a guest chef's offerings, he'd figure something out. Some of my favorite nights were the ones with no guest chef at all, because I liked making up the themes, and seeing what he'd come up with. (I'm still waiting for him to do a "Smurf 'n' Turf" night, or "The Crunch Factor.")

ANTHONY: Some of the styles/themes we offered were: Breakfast-for-Dinner, Izakaya, Fancy McDonald's, Asian Street Food, Nouveau Barbecue, Malaysian, Beer-Pairing Night, Whole-Hog Dinner, Comfort Food, Korean, Italian-American, Farm to Table, Moroccan, Pub Food, Stoner Food, Cal-Chinese, Mexiterranean, Seafood, Southern, Vegetarian, Ottoman Empire Food, Jewish, Chaat, Raw Food, Aromatics, Halloween Style, Mushroom Dinner, Egg Dinner, Vegan, and Offal. And there were plenty of others that require more explanation, like a sneak preview of a friend's new restaurant or "Miscegenation Night," which was just a snarky way to say fusion.

KAREN: In that time, we also had a lot of interesting staff come and go. Smart asses, thieves,

THE SPORTIFICATION OF FOOD

Viewed through a certain lens, Mission Street Food can look like a Food Network show brought to monstrous life: theme nights, eccentric personalities, the "extreme" environment of the Lung Shan kitchen. MSF presented a TV-worthy challenge to its guest chefs every week: *Prepare and serve an innovative small-plates menu for 150+ diners in a disorganized Chinese restaurant that will continue to serve its own take-out during your ordeal.*

For better or worse, MSF fed on and fed into the sportification of cooking, part of the transformation of a daily activity into passive entertainment, promulgated by television and embraced by America. Michael Pollan has observed that food culture in this country has shifted from the kitchen into the living room, where Americans eat processed foods in the glow of televised cooking competitions; traditional cooking shows, which demonstrated recipes and techniques, have been replaced by a lineup that educates viewers in consumerism rather than cooking. Everyone has opinions about food, and these shows have popularized a vocabulary for discussing them authoritatively. Yelp, meanwhile, has provided a forum in which diners may flourish their judgments, and then rate each others' commentary as "funny," "useful," or "cool."

Like every other restaurant in the world, MSF tempted its customers out of their kitchens, but perhaps we encouraged a particularly spectatorial orientation, as well. Our diners fashioned themselves into a panel of judges, rating dishes and comparing chefs. We often heard our customers ranking dishes on a numerical scale, or labeling the "winners" and "losers" of the meal. One regular who liked to chat with us at the cash register was particularly fond of using sports terminology; he'd praise one dish as "nothing but net" and assail another as a "brick" before moving on to football jargon to assess the rest of the food.

Of course, cooks can get pretty competitive with each other, but we tried to discourage comparisons between the home team and the visitors—that's why we never indicated which dishes came from us versus the guest chef. But in the Food Network era, it's hard to break away from the sportification of food. We may be guilty ourselves, but if we must revert to sports metaphors, then we'd rather think of MSF in terms of pro wrestling. In the end, cooking and wrestling aren't about winning and losing, so much as trash-talking and selling beer.

professional servers, and friends who needed jobs. I sometimes felt like I was more of a confessor than a manager. During service, I listened to their stories while I rang up the checks and cashed out the tips.

My real responsibilities as manager arose outside of our regular Thursday/Saturday schedule: together with Anthony, I wrote the blogs, formatted the menus, ran errands, talked with the press, and generally obsessed over Mission Street Food. We talked about the restaurant constantly. Meanwhile, I was still teaching at Berkeley. I received my Ph.D. in December 2008, and worked at Berkeley as a lecturer in Spring 2009, while MSF was taking shape.

ANTHONY: Karen's sister was expecting twins in May 2009, and Karen wanted to spend time in Oregon to help her out. We were worried about who we could trust to run the show in her absence, but at the last minute, we were able to convince one of our best friends—Sang Pahk—to relocate from Virginia and take over as manager. We trusted him implicitly, though he had no restaurant experience, little interest in food, and a questionable work ethic. An hour after we picked Sang up from the airport, of course, he got an email saying he'd been accepted to the doctoral program in sociology at the University of Hawaii, meaning he would be moving away again in August.

KAREN: I spent most of May being a good

sister in Oregon. I returned to San Francisco just in time to work an event we'd been planning for months: the Yerba Buena Center for the Arts' "Big Idea Night," which is basically a party inside a contemporary-art museum. When the YBCA invited us to cater the event, they told us to expect thousands of people, and Anthony and Sang really went for it. In the weeks leading up to that night, they prepped a ton of food and gathered materials to construct a luminescent night-market, in accordance with the museum director's vision of "22nd-century Studio 54 meets Fellini." Anthony was so stressed out about the YBCA event that his sister and brother-in-law came from Wisconsin to help out. We even rented a huge moving van to bring all the food in, and a taco truck to serve it.

Long story short, Big Idea Night was a big disaster: fuse problems, cold weather, no one eating. Instead of making a bunch of money for charity, we worked like crazy, and lost a few thousand dollars. And yet cleaning up as the sun rose the next day is still one of my favorite memories of MSF. I guess I liked the way that Anthony's sister Vicky just buckled down and did what needed to be done, in the same Myint-y way that he does.

ANTHONY: It's fun to look back on that event because I've never seen Sang work that hard, and I don't know if I've ever worked that hard myself. Then, when it turned out to be a huge failure, it wasn't even that bad because Sang was comically mad.

SOMETHING FOR EVERYONE

(Clockwise from top left)
Fried ocean trout skin; Benton's
bacon soup dumplings; the scene
inside; the line outside.

COUNTERCULTURAL CAPITAL

In the 1980s, French sociologist Pierre Bourdieu introduced the term *cultural capital* to describe assets like education and table manners, which aren't monetary, but still contribute to success and social mobility. Mission Street Food operated without a lot of restaurant-related assets—pleasant décor, comfort, privacy, good service, reasonable lighting, matching silverware—so we compensated with non-restaurant assets like irony, irreverence, and improvisation. These qualities afforded us social mobility, in the sense that we could both slum it up and dress it up, moving in either direction with impunity.

In 2010, Slavoj Žižek riffed on Bourdieu's term to produce *cultural capitalism*, which he defined as an economic system in which products are imbued with cultural capital and customers are buying the identity attached to their purchases. This is why people are willing to pay more for fair-trade chocolate—we're buying the right to think of ourselves as ethical. Mission Street Food obviously participated in the logic of cultural capitalism through our charitable agenda—among other things, diners bought the right to think of themselves as charitable.

But as a restaurant-within-a-restaurant featuring an ever-shifting menu filled with jokes about pop culture and the restaurant industry, what else were we selling at MSF? The menu item you ate and enjoyed might never be offered again, and the chef might never make another appearance. The idea of cultural capital has corporations clamoring to create an identity (at their most blatant, advertisements feature claims like "I'm a Mac" or "I'm a PC."), but Mission Street Food constantly undermined its identity, which meant we ultimately backed into a more personal relationship with our customers by way of brand destabilization. Customers were buying the right to not be told what kind of customer they were.

In essence, Mission Street Food was dealing in

MISSION STREET FOOD

July 11, 2009
Mission Stoned Food
for St. Anthony's Foundation

with guest chef Chris Ying

CHIPS AND DIP
foie french onion dip with Bugles, Cheetos, Ruffles, Pringles, Doritos, Funyuns, Hot Fries - $6.5
(veg dip available)

INVERTED NACHO
roasted corn, avocado, jalapeño crema, parmesan frico - $7

HUMBOLDT FOG
Cypress Grove goat milk nacho cheese with hash browns - $7

PB & "Js"
spicy peanut butter dipping sauce with two taquitos of duck confit and benton's bacon -or- vegetarian taquitos with banana and smoky lychee - $5

HOT POCKET
Portuguese-style chicken curry with onion, potato, and coconut milk in a fried pastry pocket - $6.5

DINNER FOR TWO FOR ONE
three-meat and ricotta meatball sandwich with tomato sauce and gruyere fonduta on homemade focaccia -and- a homemade biscuit loaded with sausage gravy - $12

PINEAPPLE EXPRESS
grilled pineapple with sweet garlic rice and crispy pancetta - $7
(veg option available)

LUNG SHAN'S VEGAN DELIGHT
shitake and oyster mushrom dumplings in miso soup - $5.5

ADDITIONS on any dish or dessert:
YOUR BRAIN ON DRUGS - $1
CRUMBLED FAMOUS AMOS - $.75
HOMEMADE RANCH - $.75

MILKY SNWIXERTEERS KAT
candy bar terrine with candied cacao and vanilla shake - $6.5

MUNCHIE SPECIAL
scoop of Humphry Slocombe's peanut butter ice cream laced with chocolate-covered pretzels - $3.50

THE GREY ALBUM (32OZ) - $7
HARD MEYER LEMONADE - $4.5
LILLET BLANC - $6 glass/$25 bottle
NEWCASTLE - $3
TECATE - $2
SODA OR BOTTLED WATER - $1
$5 CORKAGE FEE

CASH ONLY

--missionstreetfood.com

MISSION STONED FOOD

(Above) The Mission Stoned Food menu.

(Opposite page, clockwise from top) Milky Snwixerteers Kat (a terrine of assorted candy bars); tableside Famous Amos cookie-crumble service; inverted nachos (Parmesan chip, jalapeño crema, seared corn, avocado purée).

*counter*cultural capital. Never was this more evident than in July 2009, when MSF transformed into Mission Stoned Food: "a munchie space station here to rain tender morsels down on the blazed."

KAREN: Through the summer of 2009, Sang and I were co-managers of MSF, which was a lot of fun. Sang instituted some improvements in the sound system and made sure we listened to a lot more hip-hop. Then, when Michael Jackson died, he had us tuned to all MJ, all the time.

Sang stayed in an apartment across the street from us, so we saw him every day. Most Thursdays and Saturdays, he and I would meet up for sandwiches, pick up the ice cream from Humphry Slocombe, and then head in to work at MSF.

ANTHONY: That summer, I really got to know Danny Bowien, who had taken over my role as Bar Tartine's token Asian guy. Danny also obligingly took on the mantle of thorn-in-Jason's-side, since he began to use their kitchen to prep for his multiple guest-chef appearances at MSF. He completed the cycle by starting a Thursday-night pop-up restaurant on Mission Street, less than two blocks from MSF. Danny and Chris Kronner ran "Good Evening Thursday" in the second-floor "Pussycat Lounge" of an unapologetically retro-sexual bar with leopard-print carpet and stripper poles. Patrons of Good Evening Thursday ranged from hip industry kids to luminaries of California cuisine, including Alice Waters herself. (It's been called a douchefest by people other than me.)

G.E.T. had a good run selling premium steaks, Caesar salads, and Oysters Rockefeller, but it closed in August, when Chris Kronner became the executive chef at Bar Tartine. The owners wanted to take the restaurant in a more rustic direction, along the lines of their extremely successful bakery, and this decision led to an exodus of cooks from Bar Tartine. Danny headed to Europe for an eating tour, and proclaimed himself "done" with conventional fine dining. Our friend Ian Muntzert left to cook at Coi, whose kitchen is known for its technical perfection and social severity. And Jason Fox was freelancing as a consultant while weighing his options. I kept it in my head to find a way to work with those guys again.

KAREN: In August, I started a job as a visiting professor in Ohio. Anthony and I decided that MSF had too much momentum at that point for him to stop for the sake of a short-term job, so we had a long-distance marriage for the 2009–2010 school year. Meanwhile, Sang left for grad school.

During the year I was away, Anthony and I still talked about Mission Street Food a lot, but I tried to step back from the everyday operation of the business so that I could focus on being a professor. I'd give him an occasional blog edit, but that was it. Someday, I'll write a book about my Ohio adventures (the giant icicle, the heroic efforts to find vegetables, the Scottish-accented ATM), but those are all stories for later. Anthony can tell the story of the next nine months at MSF.

JASON FOX

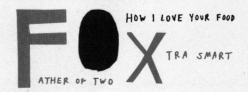

OKESTER
JA**S**O
SMOOTH OPERATOR
O**N**E
HELLUVA
CHEF
NEW JERSEY NATIVE
ARTIST

HOW I LOVE YOUR FOOD
F**O**X
XTRA SMART
FATHER OF TWO

DEAR JASON,

I CAN'T EXACTLY SAY YOU TAUGHT ME EVERYTHING I KNOW, BUT I CAN SAY THAT YOU'VE BEEN MY MENTOR IN THE KITCHEN: LEADING BY EXAMPLE, GIVING PEOPLE SPACE TO LEARN, AND MAKING FOOD THAT IS SIMULTANEOUSLY COMPLEX YET CLEAR; SOULFUL YET REFINED.

PRACTICALLY EVERY RECIPE IN THIS BOOK DRAWS ON SOME FUNDAMENTAL I LEARNED FROM YOU.

PLEASE ACCEPT THIS COLLAGE AS AN EXPRESSION OF MY THANKS FOR HELPING MISSION STREET FOOD GET OFF THE GROUND.

THANKS CHEF!
—ANTHONY

HOW'D IT GET BURNED?!

IT PUTS THE LOTION ON ITS SKIN!

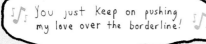

♪♪ You just keep on pushing my love over the borderline! ♪♪

1) ALWAYS GET THE MONEY UPF

2) ALWAYS LEAVE 'EM WANTING M

3) ALWAYS CHECK FOR THE ADAM

BLOGSTAURANT, FOR BETTER OR WORSE

While the restaurant industry has been pretty slow to adapt to the reality of the Internet Age, Mission Street Food was an early and enthusiastic adopter of new media. In fact, we could not have survived without the Internet. As a pop-up restaurant, we were only visible to the public for about a dozen hours a week, so we used our blog as a substitute storefront window, where we could hang our little signs—announcing upcoming events, warning that we would be closed for a wedding, or just reminding the world that we existed. We tried to keep it simple: most of our posts were just a paragraph on the next guest chef or theme, a paragraph on that night's charity, and finally, the upcoming menu. (Can we all agree that we don't need any more flash introductions, ambient electronic music, or close-up food photography before we get to see a restaurant's address?)

But the Internet is a two-way street. We had our blog and our Twitter account, but we weren't the only ones talking about MSF: we were a hot topic on local sites before we sold our first flatbread, and as time went on, we got more press from "serious" food bloggers, who took meticulous notes on the dishes they ate. Their prioritization of blogging over actually eating was, on the surface, distasteful. But upon further consideration, we started to see ourselves as equally responsible since our menus were practically begging for documentation and commentary. Even worse, we chose our themes with an eye toward our own blog. Yes, we were sellouts.

In our defense, we behaved no worse than a chef pandering to local food critics; it just so happened that our clientele was largely composed of food critics, democratically selected by themselves. Along with the food we served, we were part of an online feedback loop of blog-driven satisfaction and "critical acclaim."

Looking back, our only regret is that we spent so much time trying to make the food taste good, rather than just crafting electronic files replete with polished photos and pithy remarks ready for "consumers" to

Grocery Eats

Mission Street Food
By SergDun

Last thursday I finally made it out to Mission Street Food and it was fucking amazing. These dudes are fucking killing the game right now.

Mission Street Food is this dope project that Anthony Myint has been doing. It started with them renting one of the Antojitos San Miguel street carts every Thursday and slanging flatbread sandwiches topped with king trumpet mushroom, triple-fried potatoes, garlic confit, scallion sour cream or pork belly, jicama, pickled jalapeno and cilantro aioli. The food is super dope and hella cheap, it's fucking brilliant and no bullshit pretentious shit to any of it. Just great food. The lines at the cart were getting long so they moved it indoors. Every Thursday they now take over Lung Shan on Mission and 18th.

Last week I found out that Ryan Farr was the guest chef this week and if you've seen dude's blog you know the shit is not a game. I'd been telling myself to go but after seeing the menu I knew I had to man up.

I was won over at the chicharrones but then I saw the corned lengua. I am a fan of tongue and fuck with it any time I get a chance, although that's not always wise. Bad lengua is really fucking shitty, just imagine eating a bucket of dicks. Check Ryan's blog about how to make it, I'm going to have to try this shit because that corned tongue was better than any I've ever had. Doesn't hurt to have it served over pork belly fried rice either [...] Fuck put that shit on an english muffin and start slanging some real breakfast. Corned lengua is the fucking realest, fuck with it.

Fried Cauliflower. I've never been real big on cauliflower, as a kid I fucking hated it. I have enjoyed it since but it's not something I really check for all that much (kind of like reggae). Anyways I was amazed by this and the aioli was so nice.

[...] none of us really knew what to expect of "bacon snow" but thought it was funny so I asked for an extra gram. When we saw that it was served on a mirror well then everyone wanted to take photos of themselves snorting bacon. It got ridiculous, to the point that the waitress told us to just eat it already. Anyways Bacon Snow is the fucking truth, I will ride for that shit til the death. I know Brains was talking about bacon being the new all overprint but dude this shit brought me back. Bacon still has a long way to go. I don't know how they make it but I think it's powdered sugar infused with smoked bacon.

[...] If you're in San Francisco you really need to fuck with these Mission Street Food, it gives the chefs an avenue to boss up and just flex on food. It sucks that with the guest chef situation you only have one shot to try but quality of the food makes it so worth it. Its one of those things that really makes me love living in this city. I don't know what they have planned for the future but check their blog because you don't want to miss out on some champ food.

fuck now I'm hungry.

THE BEST REVIEW MSF EVER RECEIVED

From the blog Grocery Eats.

upload to their sites. Or perhaps we shouldn't have involved the customers at all, and simply blogged about an imaginary restaurant ourselves. Best of luck to any aspiring blogstaurateurs out there! We're looking forward to not even eating your food.

ANTHONY: It was hard losing my wife and good friend at the same time, but Karen and Sang's simultaneous departures left a void that I filled with work... and burgers. I still had the dream of starting a charitable, high-quality fast food chain, and Danny and I had spoken in passing about opening a burger stand. It was like Mission Street Food all over again—a couple of vague conversations and *poof*, we were in business. By the time Danny came back from France, most of the pieces of Mission Burger were in place. Equipment had been purchased, blogs had been published, meat had been salted, and hands had been shaken. We tested a few varieties of burgers and settled on a patty technique outlined by Heston Blumenthal, the justly celebrated chef of The Fat Duck.

In late August, after I helped Karen get settled in Ohio, Danny and I launched Mission Burger from the butcher counter of the grocery a few doors from Lung Shan. Duc Loi is a large Asian market with a substantial Latino section, plus an "isle" devoted to "American Food." I'd watched vendors come and go through the store's deli, and I approached the owner about giving it a shot myself. Amanda Ngo is one of the nicest people I've ever met—she's always friendly and community-minded—and had supported MSF with generous discounts on produce. We worked out an arrangement for Mission Burger to be open at lunch, Fridays through Wednesdays. I proposed that a dollar from each burger would go to the SF Food Bank, and she accepted without a moment's hesitation.

Mission Burger's opening menu consisted of just two items: a beef burger and a vegan burger. The beef burger was fairly true to Blumenthal's meat-column technique, but we took it a couple steps further by aging the beef before grinding it and searing the patties in beef fat (*see pages 140–143*). We also departed from his choice of homemade ketchup, home-baked brioche buns, and home-processed Emmenthal cheese—not only for logistical reasons, but also on principle. I like the classic burger accoutrements for their refreshing qualities, but I would never put that stuff on a good steak, and in my mind, the perfect burger aspires to steak-hood.

For me, caper aioli is the ideal burger condiment because its pungency highlights the beef flavor, but doesn't compete with it. We went with a mild Monterey Jack cheese, too, along with grilled onions, and *pan de mie* buns from Acme bakery. We sliced off the tops of the buns and griddled them to achieve maximum crispiness. (Side note: I still can't believe how many "gourmet" sandwiches I've had that would have been 100 percent better with 25 percent less bread.) Despite our revisions, I like to think Chef Blumenthal would have appreciated our $8 burger, which was really a $7 burger before the donation.

The vegan burger was an update on the standard garden burger, using a chickpea

panisse base and a lot of high-flavor inclusions like roasted kale and maitake mushrooms. I think it's the best veggie/vegan burger I've ever had, but we only sold it for about two months because a vegan customer objected to us frying the vegan burger in the same deep fryer as a fish-and-chips special we ran that day. She launched a negative web campaign against us. Ironically, she actually espoused the fish-and-chips place across the street as the vegan alternative to Mission Burger.

Since the vegan burger had been something of a burden to prepare anyway, we switched to a fried-chicken sandwich. We coated the chicken in vodka batter and topped it with crispy chicken skin. And after that, we made a fish sandwich with nori potato chips and aerated malt-vinegar aioli (well before every new place in town was serving that combo). But in the end, Danny just focused on refining the burger. The retirement of each sandwich brought small waves of public protest, diffused by Danny's chipper indifference. (Customers love him.)

MISSION BURGER

(Opposite page) Danny at the Duc Loi counter.

(Top) The Heston Blumenthal–inspired granulated Mission Burger.

(Center) Duc Loi Supermarket, home to Mission Burger for nine months.

(Bottom) Vodka-battered fried chicken sandwich.

THE GOLD STANDARD

by Anthony Myint

The gold standard developed in response to a need for a fixed point of comparison across different economies. Gold is not the most precious substance, but it's readily available and broadly appreciated, just like fried chicken.

So if we can all agree on fried chicken as the gold standard of food, I, in turn, submit Popeyes as the gold standard of fried chicken. And I will stand by that statement all the way to the emergency room.[1]

Of course, I support the advancement of social conventions. Modern monetary policy required a departure from the gold standard to control inflation, for example, and modern cuisine likewise benefits from advanced techniques—like sous-vide cooking to control temperature. But just as the trading of credit derivatives seems reckless in hindsight, we must regain some perspective in the realm of fried chicken.

Sorry, Chef Keller, but Ad Hoc's chicken meat wrapped in unrendered skin and crispy batter is not the ideal fried chicken (even if the meat is delicious and responsibly sourced). And in terms of price, $52/person reeks of the irrational exuberance that inevitably leads to systemic collapse. Let's remember the gold standard: Popeyes' Tuesday special is a leg and thigh for $0.99, and there's a line out the door all day long.[2]

At Mission Burger, Popeyes inspired us to push ourselves. We brined chicken thighs in spicy pickle juice, fried them in a charged vodka batter,[3] and topped them with fried chicken skins, pickled cucumbers, jalapeños, iceberg lettuce, and spicy chicken-fat mayo. It was a huge sandwich, and it was $8, of which $1 was donated to the SF Food Bank. Dedicated fans swore by it, and we sold about ten a day. We were often compared to a place in Oakland that pre-fries chicken breasts in a regular dredge hours before lunch and tops them with some parsley-and-jalapeño slaw. I've tried that sandwich, and it's a good slaw, but I can't comprehend its cult-like following (rumored to be about a thousand orders of "Fool's Gold" per day).

Perhaps the problem is that there's no food equivalent to the G-20. No one has had the authority to establish a culinary gold standard, and as a result, even experienced food professionals continue to dismiss the valuable assets passing right under their noses. A cook-friend once told me that when he brought Popeyes as a gift to the cooks of a celebrated San Francisco restaurant, the chef forbade his staff from eating it; he even condemned the precious golden nuggets as "poison."

Society may eventually move toward something more convenient than real food, just like governments began issuing paper money and credit cards. But until the proliferation of food pills and nutrient IVs, I'll measure culinary worth the old-fashioned way—at Popeyes.

---

1 My stance on Popeyes has deep roots. As my old friend Simon Huynh tells it:

One night, near the end of high school, Anthony, our friend Jin Park, and I were waiting for chicken and biscuits at Popeyes. We had requested dark meat only, and had even asked for a batch of freshly fried

chicken, though it was almost closing time. The kitchen staff was cleaning up; one employee was filling a large trash bag with fried-chicken-skin crumbs and the dark brown bits of deep fryer remains. Anthony called to the man behind the counter and asked if he could have that bag, please, since the man was just going to throw it out anyway. (Do those little deep fryer crumbs have a specific name in the restaurant industry? I don't know. For brevity, I'll call them "crispits.")

The man behind the counter looked doubtful. He poked through the crispits with tongs. "There's no meat in here," he said, as if to imply that people eat fried chicken for the sake of chicken meat. Anthony was undaunted. Finally, in a moment of weakness, the man behind the counter wondered aloud if Anthony wanted the regular crumbs or just the spicy ones, and all was lost. Ultimately a compromise was struck between Anthony, Popeyes, and the gods of common decency. The huge trash bag went to the bin and Anthony instead received a regular-sized, greasily transparent paper bag of spicy crispits. And thus we left Popeyes with the crumbly remains of the chicken fryer and our dignity.

2 Like the global economic marketplace (or public transit), the Tuesday-night Popeyes line can be a real melting pot. I've seen fights break out, but Popeyes deserves credit for being an equal-opportunity chicken broker.

3 Heston Blumenthal's technique again.

SOLID GOLD

(Opposite page) Popeyes fried chicken, bourgeois style.

(Above) Popeyes' MSG and salt–based seasoning packets, a.k.a. Cajun Sparkle.

TONY THE BUTCHER

Behind the counter at Duc Loi Market,
home of Mission Burger.

He also created a familial environment with Amanda and her employees, especially "Momma" and "Tony the butcher." I first met Momma when I was buying some chicken wings for Mission Street Food. I had placed the order early in the week, but no one had defrosted my wings, so I pulled a few of them off of an enormous frozen block of chicken ice and resigned myself to sourcing the rest elsewhere. From the checkout line, out of the corner of my eye, I saw Momma running over with two more handfuls of wings. I waved her back to the butcher counter in the hope of minimizing the salmonella threat, only to find a moment later that she was slamming the forty-pound block of frozen chicken on the ground in a desperate attempt to dislodge wings and sell me a few more. As raw chicken slid across the ground and mothers paused their strollers to take in the spectacle, it seemed like the butcher counter was all that separated the Third World from the First.

Behind her warrior-like determination, Momma turned out to be a friendly Vietnamese senior citizen who worked a paper route before work. Her partner behind the counter is Tony the butcher, who can take down three pigs in half an hour with a worn-out cleaver. In today's era of celebrity butchers, I'm proud to have worked side-by-side with a publicist-less butcher.

Tony was often grumpy about his assistants not working hard enough or about the pigs arriving late from

Chinatown, and he was extra bitchy on Monday mornings, after his day-off routine of poker and a 12-pack of Budweiser. But Danny's sunny disposition was infectious, and his staff meals helped Tony cope with the sorrows of the daily grind.

Meanwhile, Emma had taken another job, so Danny ramped up his involvement with MSF. Between Mission Burger and Mission Street Food, Danny and I were literally running back and forth between Duc Loi and Lung Shan so often that we almost bought a Segway. We soldiered on like that for a few months, discussing themes and dishes while standing around cooking burgers. I was working so much that my home electric bill went down to $8 a month—it was basically just a place to sleep. I would strategize and prep all day and then call Karen to try and strategize more with her, which is not the best way to conduct a long-distance marriage, for the record.

Up to that point, MSF had occasionally gotten by with dishes that I was not entirely happy with, but it was okay because people would think, *Hell, they're trying to butter-poach skate in a lunchbox. Let's cut them a break.* But once the novelty of MSF had worn off and guest-chef applications were at an all-time low, we felt like it was time to step it up.

In March, our friend Ian joined us at MSF, fresh off his stint at Coi. MSF had gone from just getting by with a skeleton crew, to a really strong brigade, and we wanted to get even more ambitious. But after a few weeks together with no real hierarchy, we realized that there were literally too many cooks in the kitchen. Ian was oriented toward refined California cuisine, Danny constantly pushed us to take on new techniques, and I wanted to smother everything in duck fat and guacamole. Finally, Danny proposed an elegant solution that introduced a kind of phantom executive chef to our team—we would organize our aspirations into weekly homages to culinary masters whom we admired, as if we were hosting world-famous chefs within our restaurant within a restaurant. This also gave us something to blog about.

KAREN: I only caught a couple of the homage dinners when I came back to visit, but from what Anthony told me, it seemed like those guys were creating a kind of gastronomic correspondence course. They already knew many of the techniques of haute cuisine and were constantly learning at MSF, but the homage series immersed them in research. It was the autodidact's version of weekly internships at the best restaurants in the world. They were really stretching themselves and the limits of that kitchen. On the other hand, the dining room was just as dark and dingy as it had always been, which created some cognitive dissonance when they made really fancy food. For me, in particular, it was weird to sit down as a customer at MSF and think, the more things change, the more they stay the same.

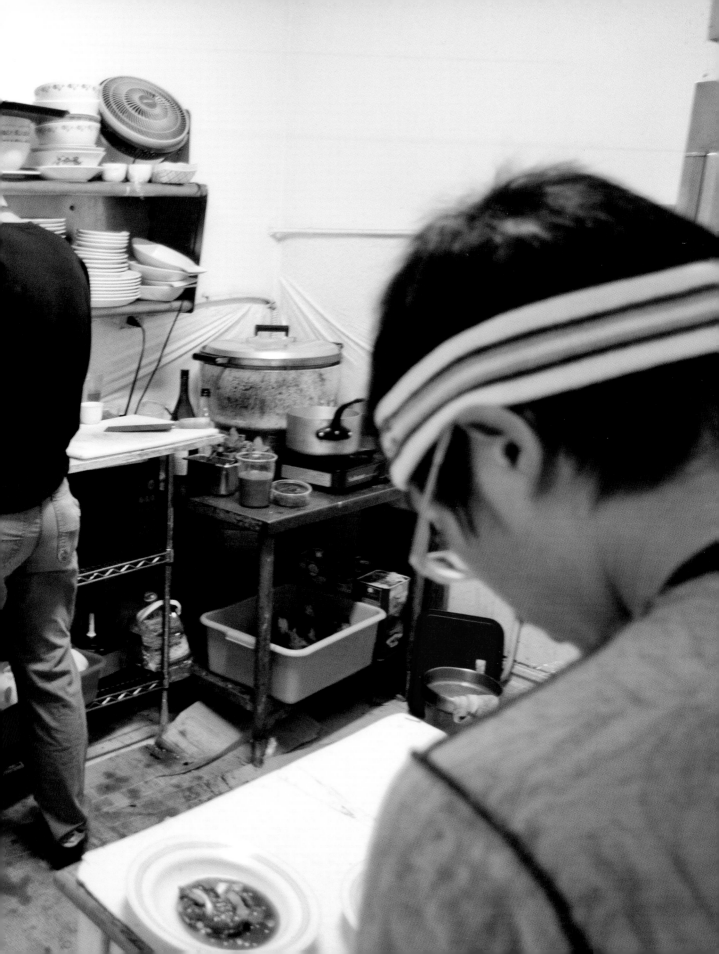

RAISING THE BAR

by Anthony Myint

Over the past half-decade, San Francisco has developed an unpleasant reputation for resting on the laurels of our incredible produce. Anecdotally, cooks in New York consider themselves superior to us because they make delicious food out of less pristine ingredients. And if you've eaten at one of the monoliths of "California cuisine," like Chez Panisse, you kind of get a sense of what they're talking about. What began as a revolutionary concept—don't adulterate great ingredients—has become established doctrine.

At one point during the course of MSF, Danny and I decided we were tired of surrendering half of our menus to "Californian" aspirations. Maybe we were being jerks, but we'd reached a point where guest-chef applications were slowing to a trickle, and invariably included flat-iron steak and an arugula salad. Meanwhile, Danny's enthusiasm, technical foundation, and disregard for the limitations of the Lung Shan kitchen would not be denied. We agreed to fully invest ourselves in each menu and put a moratorium on guest chefs. We announced our new ambitions with an inscrutable allusion to Russian pole-vaulting on our blog:

Thursday February 11th
Sergey Bubka Tribute for Groceries for Seniors

Sergey Bubka is to pole vault what Usain Bolt would be to sprinting if no one breaks those records for 25 years (and if Usain Bolt was white).

From 1984 to 1988, Bubka increased the world record 21 cm and is still the reigning world record holder by 9 cm. According to Gary Smith of Sports Illustrated, *"Here is a man who has personally altered his art form, changed the way competitors prepare for it and perform it, even the way spectators perceive it." This Thursday, guest chef Danny Bowien pays tribute to the all-time great, with a seafood-driven menu inspired by Bubka's accomplishments—literally.*

Aperitif—prosecco, raspberry, black sesame - $4

Katsuo Boullion—braised hamachi collar, turnip brûlée, nori tamago, pickled turnip greens - $8

Tasmanian Ocean Trout Sashimi—roe "en escabeche," Santa Barbara sea urchin, crispy rice paper, dill - $12

Salad of Radishes and Sprouts—smoked eel, golden enoki, crushed peas, radish water, tarragon, horseradish - $7

Lightly Grilled Littleneck Clams—smoked habañero shoyu, pineapple vinegar, olive-oil puffed barley - $8

Gambas a la Sal—whole shrimp baked in sea salt, burnt eggplant, squash caviar, lemon confit - $9

Oysters on the Half-shell—pulled pork shoulder, poached napa cabbage, salt pickles, spicy whole bean miso - $13

Fig on a Plate[1]—fig and honey parfait with oolong ice milk, mint, walnut tuille - $6

Thus, we laid down the gauntlet for ourselves. No more pseudo-rustico-Italian cuisine based around seasonal produce. A few months later, we decided to kick a dead horse, and address the shortcomings of the term "California cuisine" directly. Ian had already worked in three of the actual restaurants we would be referencing, so we were confident we could paint a fair portrayal of the two schools of California cooking.

Saturday May 29th
California Cuisine: A Case Study

As an epilogue to our recent homage series, this Saturday we'll be examining California cuisine by preparing food in the style of some notable area restaurants which represent two approximate schools of thought: innovation and simplicity. Included will be dishes in the style of Ubuntu, Zuni Cafe, The French Laundry, Delfina, Manresa, Nopa, Commis, and Chez Panisse.

Chilled Pea Consomme, with White Chocolate and Macadamia Nuts - $6 (pictured above)

Caesar Salad - $7

"Oysters & Pearls"—Oysters, Tapioca, Caviar - $12

Spaghetti with Tomato Sauce - $8

A Spring Tidal Pool with Octopus, Sea Urchin and Abalone - $15

Vegetable Tagine - $9

Pork Jowl, Slow Egg, Potato, Black Garlic, Alliums - $12

Assortment of Fresh Fruit from the Market - $6

---

1 This was a reference to a remark by David Chang in 2009, dismissing California cuisine as nothing more than "serving figs on a plate." San Franciscans were indignant, but embarrassingly, not long before, one of the city's premier restaurants was serving an uncut nectarine lolling around on a plate as a dessert for $8.

ANTHONY: To prepare for the homage dinners, Danny, Ian, and I would use the Internet to ogle menus and haute-cuisine blogs for hours (which those guys were doing in their spare time, anyway). Ultimately, the series felt gratifying and deflating at the same time. When we'd see a complex and exotic dish and then try to make it with locally available ingredients in our own pedestrian kitchen, we'd feel proud, but also a little less excited to try the real thing—some of the magical naiveté had vanished. For me, the bubble literally burst in the case of *poulard en vessie*, a truffled chicken steamed in a pig's bladder. I'm sure that Bresse chickens and Périgord truffles would significantly improve matters, but having forced forty chickens into bladder holes, I'm afraid I'll never recapture my youthful innocence.

It was around this time that Karen started wondering out loud how long we could sustain Mission Street Food, since it was "like planning a wedding twice a week." It's true: we were constantly trying to reinvent ourselves, and you can't do that forever. Eventually, I felt like we were "faking the funk," or at least feeling less inspired, and it was probably better to end on a high note. After all, as I learned from Jason Fox, you should always leave 'em wanting more. Plus, by mid-2010, scores of unconventional restaurants had "popped up." It was time to try something new.

Mission Street Food ended on June 5th, 2010, after 139 nights, 70 guest chefs, and over $35,000 raised for various causes. In its twenty-month run, we'd accumulated a significant amount of good will, and we rolled that over into some financing and enthusiasm for a new restaurant, which we started in the spot that we'd initially wanted for Mission Street Food, just two doors down from Lung Shan. Back when Karen and I were first looking for a place to sublet on Thursdays, the owner of El Herradero taquería had declined our proposal to share her space, but after a year of seeing a line out the door at MSF, she offered to sell us her restaurant so she could retire. I had always liked the idea of having a freestanding building with a parking lot, and I liked the sunny feel of the dining room.

MSF HOMAGE DINNERS

(Opposite page, left to right)

Olive oil cake, crème fraîche ice cream, strawberry, aged balsamic (Pascal Barbot).

Sea urchin, cucumber, frozen cream, dill granita (René Redzepi).

Poulard en Vessie: game hen and black truffles steamed in pig's bladder (Auguste Escoffier).

Gargouillou: a variety of vegetables, herbs and seeds prepared appropriately (Michel Bras).

Miso-poached foie gras with legumes (Inaki Aizpitarte).

Roasted beets, young goat cheese, olive soil, and chickweed (Bras).

Bison tartare, tarragon, oyster, juniper, sorrel (Redzepi).

A Basic Understanding of Lamb: roasted leg, braised belly, assorted seeds, and grains (QuiQue Dacosta).

Skate, ramps, vegetable stems, mussel sauce (Redzepi).

HOMAGE DINNER SERIES: NOMA

by Anthony Myint

During the last few weeks of Mission Street Food, we decided to do away with guest chefs and center our menus around the menus of phantom culinary heroes. But since we didn't have the resources or connections to actually visit any of the restaurants we were mimicking, we had to piece together our recipes by poring over images online and culling bits of information here and there, not unlike teenagers learning about sex from porn.

To provide a little bit of insight into our process, I'll lay out the days leading up to an homage to Copenhagen's Noma and its chef, René Redzepi. In case you're unfamiliar with it, Noma earned the #1 spot in 2010's San Pellegrino World's 50 Best Restaurants list. Without getting too starry-eyed, let's just say that René Redzepi has probably created the world's most successful combination of high technique with locally sourced products, and redefined Nordic cuisine.

But to put things in context, Noma usually serves about thirty people per night. At MSF, we were preparing to serve 100 to 150. Noma has a staff that fluctuates between twenty and thirty people, depending on how many unpaid interns they have. Meanwhile, we had a staff of four, two of whom had other full-time jobs. We were feeling our way in the dark, with one hand tied behind our backs. Of course we didn't produce food of the caliber served at Noma, but we were proud to learn by doing, and in our audacious spirit, we felt like we were doing right by Chef Redzepi.

Dish

SEA URCHIN, FROZEN CREAM, CUCUMBER, DILL GRANITA

SHAVED WATER CHESTNUT, WALNUT, COD ROE, RYE CRISP

MACKEREL CRUDO, GRILLED DAIKON, HORSERADISH SNOW

SPOT PRAWN WITH SEAWATER AND PARSLEY EMULSION

SALSIFY, MILK SKIN, TRUFFLE

SKATE, RAMPS, VEGETABLE STEMS, MUSSEL SAUCE

VEAL SWEETBREAD, CAULIFLOWER CREAM, ONION, ELDERBERRY VINAIGRETTE

YOGURT PARFAIT, PEAS, CELERY, CHERVIL, PEA SHOOTS, MINT OIL

OLLEBROD (FRESH CHEESE ICE CREAM, FROTHED MILK, BEER-SOAKED RYE BREAD)

Prep notes	Assessment
Blended dill with salt, sugar, and water. Froze it, then scraped it. Froze cream and scraped it. Deduced from online photos that Redzepi coated cucumber in vegetable ash. Charred vegetable scraps over wok burner, then pulsed ashy bits to create a powder. Plated with sea urchin and picked dill.	Overall, I was satisfied with our approximation of the techniques, although the respective salt-acid balances were not fine-tuned.
Peeled and shaved fresh water chestnut. Made a dressing from cod roe with cream and olive oil. Shaved dark rye bread on a deli slicer and toasted it. To assemble, made compositions of shavings perched against each other with dollops of cod roe dressing and walnuts interspersed.	This was a fairly weak approximation. I don't think our rye crisps or the cod roe vinaigrette were very good.
Butchered and cured mackerel in a mix of salt, water, and vinegar. For the daikon, grilled large pieces and then shaved wispy sheets with one grilled edge. For horseradish snow, used Jason Fox's method of microplaning, freezing, and then pulsing the frozen shreds in the blender.	This dish was very good, and I think we offered a reasonable approximation of a relatively simple dish.
Supplier fell through, forcing us to resort to frozen sushi-grade prawns. Redzepi serves dish on large rocks. Went to a landscaping company, sorted through slate rubble. Blended parsley, wakame, and agar for emulsion. Pictures depicted unnamed purple powder. Took a stab at it with ground Pacific dulse.	This came out all right, but using frozen prawns was discouraging. We also later learned that Redzepi blends oysters into his purée, which undoubtedly makes it better.
Ordered a pound of relatively cheap Himalayan truffles and blended along with truffle oil and mushroom stock. Poached salsify in milk until tender. For the milk skins, gathered the surface layer from a pot of warm milk, repeatedly. Lightly caramelized salsify and enrobed it with milk skin.	Given the volume we needed and the number of other projects we were trying to finalize, the milk skins were a source of considerable stress, but very delicious.
Cooked mussels. Shucked and puréed them. Folded the purée into fresh aioli with additional lemon juice. Cleaned and cut chard and kale stems along with turnip greens. Cooked and shocked them. Poached skate filets in beurre monté to order. Served with sauce, greens, and ramps.	The richness of the mussels and the pungency of the ramps provided a nice contrast. I'm curious about how Redzepi actually does it.
Parcooked sweetbreads by gently poaching. Cooked cauliflower in cream, then puréed it with the reduced cream. Blanched individual shallot and onion leaves. Rehydrated dried elderberries in Banyuls vinegar, added pomegranate juice and olive oil. Crisped flour-dusted sweetbreads in brown butter.	We did an okay job with this, with the exception of the vinaigrette—it was an error to use dried elderberry, which sullied the dish with a potpourri-like dried-floral quality.
Made buttermilk panna cottas (see pages 200–201). Would've liked to experiment with yogurt parfait, but time limitations called for the safe route. Blanched, shocked, and blended mint with grapeseed oil, then strained through a coffee filter. Served panna cottas with small spring-vegetable forest.	Some guests claimed that this was one of the best desserts they'd ever had. I think we really gained some insight into Redzepi's refined use of vegetable flavors in desserts.
Soaked rye croutons in a mix of Chimay and wheat beer. Served each dish with a quenelle of crème fraîche ice cream. Added lecithin to sweetened raw milk. Blended the milk and skimmed the froth to serve.	This dish didn't quite come together, in part because the contrast between the components wasn't extreme enough and resulted in a slightly homogenous combination.

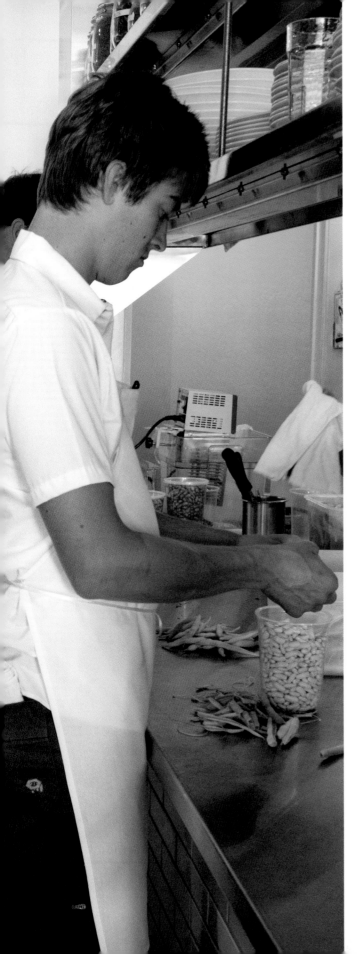

With El Herradero on my mind, I approached my old friends from Bar Tartine to see if they would want to partner with me. After months of discussions and fundraising, the plan started to take shape. Jason Fox and Ian Muntzert would be executive chef and chef de cuisine, respectively, while Bar Tartine's ex–general manager Xelina Leyba would take the front-of-the-house reins again. We were getting the old band back together! For me, the biggest draws were that the daily operations would be stable, everyone was committed to sustaining a benevolent business model, and I knew I would be proud to be part of any restaurant run by Jason, Ian, and Xelina. We broke ground in March 2010, and five months later, Commonwealth Restaurant opened for business.

Around the same time that Mission Street Food closed, Danny and I ended Mission Burger. We'd served about 5,000 burgers in nine months, which may not seem like a lot compared to Mickey D's, but it was usually just one of us behind the counter, and we were only open a few hours a day. On the last day of business,

COMMONWEALTH

Finishing up the final construction touches, while the kitchen rounds out its menu.

COMMONWEALTH

"A fundamental shift is occurring in the restaurant business, with chefs producing serious food in casual surroundings. And Commonwealth is the pacesetter."

—San Francisco Chronicle

"These exciting and luscious dishes give us a thrillingly high experience at approachable prices."

—San Francisco Examiner

"... the most exciting new venture of the year... a restaurant that feels both worldly and distinctly local, a departure from the norm that reads like a promising sign of what lies ahead." —San Francisco Magazine

While we'd like to think that you could've said the same things about Mission Street Food, no one did. Commonwealth bears almost no resemblance to MSF. Commonwealth's dining room is sophisticated and minimal, the waitstaff are synchronized and polished, and the kitchen is state-of-the-art and spotless. Parties are seated at their own tables. The plates match, and the appetizers precede the entrées. Diners are, for the most part, confident they're in the right place.

And yet some of the underlying values remain. As the name implies, Commonwealth is charitable: we donate ten dollars from every tasting menu to good causes, with beneficiaries changing on a monthly basis. The name also speaks to accessible bounty—we all wanted to create a fine-dining restaurant without a stuffy atmosphere or steep prices. As general manager, Xelina Leyba creates an atmosphere that critic Josh Sens called "debonair but laid-back," which evidently some people prefer to the "chaotic but cramped" confines of Mission Street Food.

Jason Fox and Ian Muntzert are putting out small and medium plates with a playful relationship to ingredients and culinary traditions. They're more consistent and refined than we ever hoped to be. (But in all fairness to MSF, much less of Commonwealth's kitchen resources are devoted to producing General Tso's chicken.)

At this point, it seems like most of Commonwealth's customers have never heard of Mission Street Food, and that's the way we want it. There are little traces of "street" heritage around the restaurant, but we've been trying to hide or cover them up (although people probably wonder what's going on when they step into the bathroom and see enormous Chinese propaganda posters). The truth is that Commonwealth is a reflection of Jason, Ian, and Xelina—but we're happy to accept compliments on their behalf.

Danny single-handedly sold 125 burgers in three hours. And ever since we stopped cooking at Duc Loi, friends and strangers alike have approached me to reminisce about the Mission Burger. Regardless of how we might disagree about politics or worldly issues, it's nice to know that we're united by that basic connection—just a bunch of sweaty beasts roaming the earth in search of a nice granulated patty.

Karen returned home in May, just in time for one last burger, and in June, we all went to Danny's wedding in Seoul. Danny's wife, Youngmi Mayer, used to live in Korea, and her family showed us a good time, both in the city and at her parents' house in the country. After a month off for travel and leisure, we returned to San Francisco to start another restaurant from the ashes of MSF.

On July 5th, 2010, Mission Chinese Food was born, eight years to the day after Lung Shan Restaurant first opened. Whereas Mission Street Food had sublet a space from Lung Shan a couple times a week, Mission Chinese Food partnered directly with the Liangs to serve our food for lunch and dinner every day, and to deliver it all over the city. We would serve the kind of food we wanted to eat: spicy, creative Chinese food made with high-quality ingredients and the techniques we'd learned from fine dining (and at MSF).

Once again, we threw ourselves out of the frying pan and into the wok burner. After countless unpredictable nights at Mission Street Food, it seemed like selling a little Chinese food would be a cakewalk, but I've never seen Sue's stoic face contort into a grimace like it did on the first night of Mission Chinese Food. You'd really think we hadn't learned a damn thing since the first night of MSF. For some reason, we had Youngmi working by herself answering phones and waiting tables for a venture that was publicized by every food journalist in the city. Equally inexplicably, we had thought that delivery would be a snap. A number of friends who wandered in for dinner that night (Karen, Carlo Espinas, Chris Ying, and Chris Crawford) saw what was going on, strapped on aprons, and didn't stop working until we closed at 11 p.m.

But as with all shitshows, it was a learning experience, and among other things, we learned about "the hotline." Part of the reason for the understaffing on opening night was Sue's confidence that if we needed to hire more cooks, we need only call "the hotline" and we'd have a cook in two hours. Unconfirmed rumors and speculation suggest that "the hotline" is an informal gray-market subsector of the Chinatown unemployment office—a more organized and systematic version of the parking lots and street corners where Latinos wait to be hired as day-laborers.

By noon on Day Two, we had some applicants. Apparently, the Chinese interview process goes something like this:

MISSION CHINESE FOOD

Ma Po Tofu.

SUE: Where do you live?

APPLICANT: Mission and Fourteenth.

SUE: Okay. *CAN YOU DO THE JOB?*

APPLICANT: Uh, yeah.

SUE: Okay. Can you start in an hour?

We encountered a twist on the standard interview process later that afternoon, when a guy, his mother, and his grandmother showed up for the same job and asked us to pick one of them.

This was how we began our relationship with a beefy twenty-six-year-old whom Danny nicknamed "T-Bone." He'd been in the U.S. for only two weeks, and spoke virtually no English, but T-Bone was immediately indispensable. His consistency and skill allowed Danny the freedom to carve out new, stronger MCF menus. We later learned that he attended a dim-sum school for two years. One of our most taxing operational stretches was when he took a couple weeks off to get married in China (and to get a micro-perm, evidently).

The food at MCF spanned China's provinces, with an emphasis on Szechuan cuisine, but we employed techniques from a variety of culinary traditions. We characterized the new venture as "Americanized Oriental Food" on our blog—a phrase I suggested as a compromise with Danny, who wanted to name the whole endeavor "Mission Oriental Food." Though the term "Oriental" sparked some controversy, we weren't trying to be provocative—Danny was just making a nostalgic reference to his childhood in Oklahoma, where "Oriental" had been in common use. In order to diffuse some of the public outrage, I played the race card, calling it a commentary on culinary Eurocentrism and citing our "Eastern" backgrounds.

Mission Chinese Food was anything but a gimmicky publicity stunt, though. Cooks like to cook for other cooks, and to serve up bad-ass food. Most cooks I know love Chinese food. I may be biased, but it's hard to think of a more bad-ass accomplishment as a chef than going into a shitty kitchen in which no one speaks your language, or shares your fundamental approach to cooking, and producing food that has locals sitting side by side with culinary hotshots and foodies on pilgrimages from New York, L.A., and overseas. I'm also proud to run a restaurant in which Chinese moms and grandmas listen to Biggie, serve refined Szechuan dishes for $9, deliver it around the city, and still send bi-weekly checks to the SF Food Bank.

At this point, I've relinquished any claim to the title of chef and fully inhabit my new role as consultant/hype-man/busboy, which actually makes pretty good use of my natural talents. As chef, Danny has developed a tighter bond with the people at Lung Shan than I ever could, even though he's just starting to pick up a few Cantonese words here and there. It's touching to see Danny create a more interactive family dynamic than we had before, with the staff exchanging back rubs and thumbs-up signs. It's like the foreign-film effect, where the language barrier clouds critical analysis enough for the charm of the human condition to shine through.

As with a real family, there have been occasional rough stretches. Since we've entered into a closer partnership with Lung Shan, there've been shouting matches over beers comped for friends and too-expensive tomatoes, and difficult conversations about taxes and making ends meet. On several occasions, both Sue and Danny have suggested calling it quits. But also like a real family, everyone has too much history and emotional investment to let it all go; we've chosen to forgive and forget. Every time Mission Chinese Food has gotten to the verge of collapse, we've renewed everyone's enthusiasm with another crackpot project.

And so, after the umpteenth argument about the cost of using all-natural meat, we decided that an ambitious-yet-cheap remodel would boost morale. We spent the next few days wallpapering, framing the massive Communist propaganda posters that lined the walls, installing new lighting, and building a dumpling station in the front window. And when we needed another spiritual pick-me-up, we started a public fundraiser for an enormous illuminated Chinese New Year's Dragon. When the beast arrived, it finally felt like we were putting down roots, even if those roots reached into the ceiling.

ORIENTALISM

by Karen Leibowitz

At its best, the scene at Lung Shan was a study in multicultural togetherness—a hippie commune offering language classes and promoting the free exchange of ideas. At its worst, it was an irreconcilably heterogeneous jumble—Asian-American chefs intruding in the kitchen and hipster youths packing the sleepy dining room.

In the two years that Mission Street Food shared space with Lung Shan Restaurant, four Chinese men passed through the kitchen as cooks for the restaurant's regular menu. We never knew their given names—we just referred to each of them as *shifu*. The French word *chef* literally means "chief" or "boss"; similarly, the Cantonese word *shifu* can be applied to kung fu experts, cabbies, and other masters of their own domains. It's the normal way of addressing a head cook.

The first shifu was a grump; he clearly resented our presence, and he didn't stay long after we arrived. The next shifu was much friendlier. We marveled at his ability to flip massive pans of egg foo young, and he seemed happy to trade cooking skills with us—showing off his moves on the wok and watching amusedly as we baked pastries in Lung Shan's small, rickety oven.

But one Saturday afternoon, this mild-mannered shifu stormed out of the kitchen. He said that Anthony had told the guest chef to *Watch out for that guy. He's a dangerous cook.* Given that Shifu spoke no English, the incident seemed to be a projection of his own feelings about sharing the kitchen with outsiders. Shifu's voice rose into a shout as he recounted a series of paranoid translations of English expressions, and everyone realized that he'd been storing up resentments for months. (Later, when Anthony asked Sue's mother to explain what happened, she said simply, *Dai yee ngow*—He's a big-eared bull, i.e., he's stubborn.) Sue tried to reason with Shifu, then shouted after him as he walked out, right before the dinner rush. The third shifu arrived the next day.

This shifu was wrinkled and smiley. During his reign, MSF introduced a cooperative dish called "Lung Shan's Vegan Delight"—a shiitake-dumpling soup, designed by Anthony, prepped by Sue's mother, and cooked by Shifu. When an order came in, the server would tell Anthony, and he would relay it to Shifu. Sometimes Anthony was busy in another part of Lung Shan's labyrinthine kitchen, so he taught me to order soup in Cantonese. Gradually, I learned to order up to five bowls of soup, say please and thank you, and distinguish the total number of soups from the number of new orders coming in. I'd poke my head into the back kitchen and shout my order over the noise of the woks. Shifu would grin and nod, holding up the appropriate number of fingers to indicate he'd gotten the message. I'd nod back, mirroring his fingers.

When I came back to MSF after a few months in Ohio, I shouted an order toward the back. I looked up for confirmation, and saw a surprised-looking middle-aged Chinese guy. (All the shifus were middle-aged Chinese guys, by the way.) It was the new shifu, whom I'd never met. The fourth shifu is still cooking at Lung Shan, but in the last year, the line between the two operations has become much blurrier.

When Mission Street Food reinvented itself as Mission Chinese Food in 2010, we created a socio-culinary conundrum: Chinese guys cooking Americanized Chinese food, Asian-American hipsters cooking Sino-American food, and American customers asking for Tsingtao with pronunciations of ambiguous provenance. CONTINUED ON PAGE 110

The first signature item on the Mission Chinese Food menu serves nicely as an allegory for Mission Street Food's ongoing identity struggles. The "chinito" was a dish riffing on a dim sum classic, *zhaliang*—Chinese donuts[1] wrapped in a wide rice noodle. Anthony stuffed zhaliang with duck confit, cucumber, and spicy hoisin to produce an appetizer that's crunchy yet slippery, and savory yet sweet, like the offspring of a mixed marriage between zhaliang and Peking duck. The name was not only an abbreviation of "Chinese burrito," but also a mildly derogatory term for Asians, meaning something like "little Chinaman" in Spanish.

This made some people uncomfortable. When we were an "American" restaurant, part of our identity was built around disparity: *Lung Shan is a Chinese restaurant, but on Thursdays and Saturdays, it becomes Mission Street Food, and serves a different menu.* But now that we're Mission Chinese Food, the distinction is murky.

It seemed to demand some sort of commentary from us. But when we characterized the new business as "Americanized Oriental Food," comments on the Internet ranged from liberal pleading (*"Be a little more PC please! the term oriental has some very derogatory history attached to it, equivalent to the n-word"*) to self-righteous mudslinging (*"Do these d-bags even know the historically racist significance of the word Oriental?"*[2]) and, in a few rare cases, support (*"They're Asian themselves. It was tongue-in-cheek. Calm down"*).

In any case, our use of "Oriental" had been a compromise: Danny had lobbied to call the whole thing "Mission Oriental Food." Plus, picking such a pointed identifier seemed like an amusing way to acknowledge the irony and confusion inherent in our situation.

Incidents like these produce an undesirable level of introspection in a restaurant. We wonder, for instance, whether Anthony has a greater right to experiment with Chinese food than cooks who aren't ethnically Chinese. Does it matter that Danny is Asian-American if he's still thoroughly foreign to the Chinese people at Lung Shan (whose Cantonese nickname for him is "Korean guy"). Why are online reviewers so obsessed with establishing their personal identity as the basis from which they judge our food ("*As an Asian-American...*")?

Mission Chinese Food is only one incarnation of an evolving business that has never had a clear ethnic label. We began with a Chinese-Burmese-American and a Jewish-American moonlighting in a Guatemalan taco truck, with help from Filipino-American, Chinese-American, and Filipino-Chinese-American friends. We only got more confusing from there, as we hired Asian-American, Latin-American, African-American, and Caucasian-American staff to run around a Chinese restaurant, serving food from Europe, Asia, the Middle-East, Latin America, California, or wherever. In fact, a lot of the people and foods came from more than one place. This is not meant as an inspirational story about diversity—it just shows how complicated and inadequate geographical terms are in descriptions of people and food alike.

We feel authorized to make dishes outside our families' ethnic traditions, and we freely mix different cultures' ingredients and techniques, because we like to eat delicious food, wherever it comes from. After a while, sticking with "authentic" food from your own identity is boring. (Especially if you're Jewish.)

THE COOKS OF MISSION CHINESE FOOD

(Page 109) Shifu #4 catching a few winks between orders.

(Opposite page) From T-Bone's wedding album.

(Above) Danny Bowien, Oklahoma-raised, Korean-American Chinese food wizard.

---

1 In Cantonese, these donuts are called *you tiao*; literally, "oil stick." Like so many Chinese words, that's brutally accurate, but they're no oilier than any other donuts. Think of them as big unglazed crullers.

2 In his seminal 1978 book, *Orientalism*, Edward Said described an imperialist pattern of thought that grouped Arab and Asian cultures under the rubric of "the Orient," which was larded with descriptors premised on presumed difference from and opposition to European culture. After publishing *Orientalism*, Said developed his theory of representations of the cultural "other" to acknowledge the range of assimilation between "East" and "West"; in *Culture and Imperialism* (1993), Said focused on the "contrapuntal" experience of cultural contact, arguing that "Orientalist" perspectives are flawed largely because they obscure cultures' impact on one another, particularly in the United States. "[...] American identity is too varied to be a unitary and homogenous thing; indeed the battle within it is between advocates of a unitary identity and those who see the whole as a complex but not reductively unified one. [A]ll cultures are involved in one another; none is single and pure, all are hybrid, heterogenous, extraordinarily differentiated, and unmonolithic" (xxv). In referring to Mission Chinese Food as a purveyor of "Americanized Oriental Cuisine," we were drawing on Said's sense of orientalism as a flattening of varied experience into a single image that can be consumed, judged, and managed without upsetting the structure of "us" versus "them."

THE DRAGON

*Community funding brought this
60-foot spectacle from Beijing to the
Mission Chinese Food dining room.*

In a lot of ways, the dragon embodies our approach to what we do—it's less about filling people's stomachs than about nourishing a sense of possibility. (And less about pleasing everyone than about keeping ourselves happy.) We could serve the same food on white table-cloths and keep our donations for ourselves, but that would feel soulless. Instead, we're focused on the kind of community that's built by sharing a meal, a space, or an experience.

Mission Street Food no longer exists, and I'm already nostalgic about Mission Chinese Food, the way I imagine a father must feel about

his child growing up. My own father never understood what I was doing with my life, even though it was largely inspired by his example. Then again, he would have had a heart attack if he knew I was eating pork, so maybe it's better that we never discussed PB&Js. Besides, the whole thing is hard to explain: after everything that Mission Street Food has been through, we're left with a Chinese restaurant that now sells Chinese food, a fine-dining restaurant run by people who used to run a nearby fine-dining restaurant, some Internet bloat—and this book.

We know that a lot of our experiences at Mission Street Food were plain luck, but we still hope the story inspires someone with a bit of willfulness and naiveté to chase their own dragon.

PART THREE
THE FOOD

Decision-making is more
important to cooking
than exact amounts,
temperatures, or times.

GENERAL THOUGHTS ON COOKING

There's more than one way to skin a catfish. You can slice it with a knife, tug it with pliers, or just get someone else to do it. And these "techniques" actually represent the three fundamental approaches cooks can follow: finesse, brute force, and outsourcing.

All cooks—professional and recreational alike—would love to finesse everything, but finesse takes time. Brute force and outsourcing are convenient, but are often synonymous with lower quality. While sometimes it makes sense to use finesse and brunoise your garlic, other times it makes sense to use brute force and just throw it in a food processor. I would never outsource minced garlic, but I am in favor of outsourcing ingredients like pomegranate juice or Twinkies, which are best left to specialists.

Mission Street Food involved a constant shortage of manpower, equipment, time, and space. Combined with numerous completely new tasks each week, our standard operating procedure was to reexamine the tradeoffs of each approach and try to find an optimal mix. Of course, menu changes aren't unique to Mission Street Food. Plenty of restaurants change their menus on a daily basis, according to the availability of ingredients or simple whim. But for us, it wasn't just a matter of mak-

ing seasonal variations on Mediterranean food; it was curing lardo and wrapping it around asparagus tempura one night, and making harissa vinaigrette and scraping young coconuts for a salad with mango, chicory, and Oaxacan cheese the next.

Goofy as it might sound, serving themed food for a single night in a dive restaurant is the kitchen equivalent of improvisational comedy. It might not always be polished or reliable, but that kind of controlled chaos can also produce some moments of unexpected inspiration. The constraints of MSF forced us to think about how we cook, and how to streamline fine-dining methods so that they could be executed in a cruddy kitchen with limited manpower—much like the constraints of the average home kitchen. (No offense to yours.)

This section consists of our ideas about the ideal balance between finesse, brute force, and outsourcing, and about how you can reap the benefits of fine-dining methods while keeping things manageable and affordable. What I want to convey is that decision-making is more important to cooking than exact amounts, temperatures, or times. This is how we approached the constantly changing requirements of the MSF kitchen, and it's how we think home cooking is best

approached, as well. And so, this section will feature general principles and philosophies more than specific recipes, though some professional kitchen terms will be included so you can sound credible if you talk to a line cook about this stuff.

What follows will not impress every chef out there, but it should provide enough techniques and insights to help most people approach fine dining and/or improve their cooking. Before MSF, Danny Bowien, Ian Muntzert, and I spent years in some of San Francisco's top kitchens, building a strong technical foundation in both traditional cooking and molecular gastronomy; during the year and a half in which we opened our kitchen to guests, we worked with more than seventy different chefs, observing their ideas and methods. These are the CliffsNotes. The ideas here are all mainly based on one of three general tactics: 1) adding a level of flavor and/or refinement to simpler foods, 2) cherry-picking the most worthwhile concepts in haute cuisine, or, 3) introducing or recommending an efficient approach. Not everyone has dedicated their lives to the pursuit of cuisine, but most people wouldn't mind eating and cooking better, and these are some useful fundamentals.

A QUICK GUIDE TO USEFUL CUTS OF BEEF AND PORK

CUTS	PREPARATION	COST	NOTES
Beef ribeye, New York strip, tenderloin	Cook to temp	$$$ – $$$$	Ribeye is fatty, and the most flavorful cut. NY strip is beefy and lean. Filet is the most tender, but the most expensive.
Beef hanger, flap steak, sirloin	Cook to temp	$ – $$$	Hanger and flap have good flavor, but are generally chewier than the premium steaks listed above.
Beef cheek, brisket, chuck	Slow and low	$ – $$	Cheek has the most fat and collagen, and so it's the most tender, but it's harder to find.
Beef short rib and oxtail	Slow and low	$$ – $$$	Tasty cuts that end up being a little pricey after you factor in bone weight.
Beef tongue	Slow and low	$$	Tender, squidgy texture. Lends itself well to portioning/slicing once cooked.
Pork chop, loin, tenderloin	Cook to temp	$ – $$	Mild in flavor. Easy to overcook. Tenderloin is usually worth the slightly higher price, if your butcher has it.
Pork spare rib, back rib	Slow and low	$ – $$	Spare ribs are cheap and meaty, but have huge fatty sections, too. Back ribs have a desirable, flaky muscle pattern and a consistent distribution of fat.
Pork cheek, shoulder	Slow and low	$	Fairly meaty and affordable.
Pork jowl, belly	Slow and low	$	Extremely fatty cuts. Jowl meat is gelatinous with large sections of fat, whereas belly has more striated, interspersed layers of meat and fat. Both are indulgences.

MEATS

Meat is usually the most expensive ingredient you'll use, so it's a good starting point for planning. It would be impractical to buy filet mignon so you could grind it and stew it, and buying a chuck roast only to cut it into steaks and cook it to medium rare would leave you chewing until the cows come home. The above chart indicates which cuts should be cooked relatively quickly, to a specific internal temperature, and which should be cooked at a low temperature for a long time. Within the cells in the first column, the types of cut are listed from least to most expensive, with notes on particular characteristics. The chart is not exhaustive: many cuts of

SALTING AND AGING STEAK

(From left to right) Day Zero, straight from the package; Day One; and Day Two of a broken-down and salted ribeye's aging process.

meat are omitted, because the listed cuts offer better value/quality, in my opinion. (For example, flank steak is not on the chart because it costs as much as sirloin but is less tender, while hanger and flap steak are about as good as flank steak but cost less.) Other cuts are not mentioned because you can often extrapolate from what's here. (For example, lamb shoulder should be cooked slowly at a low temperature, just like pork shoulder.)

Cooking To Temperature

The process of cooking meats to a specific internal temperature isn't complicated or novel, but it's worth outlining the steps that elevate it from amateur to professional results: salting, tempering, cooking, and resting.

Salting: Buy meat at least one day in advance. Red meat is typically flavorful enough that salting is preferable to brining or marinating. Premium steakhouses build flavor by aging beef for a month or more in controlled environments, then trimming off a lot of the exterior meat, which will have acquired an inedible moldy layer.

I endorse a relatively common method of "quick aging" that can accomplish some of the same enzymatic improvement in a regular refrigerator, without the waste. I like to salt red meat and leave it uncovered on a cooling rack in the fridge for at least a day, and up to three days. The color will deepen, so that after Day One, the meat will be crimson. After Day Two it will be dark red; and on Day Three, reddish-brown. Basically you're trying to draw out excess water and concentrate flavor.

Pork, chicken, and other white meats can be salted, or—since they are milder in flavor—marinated. Cookbooks conventionally recommend brining pork and chicken, but brining presents a trade-off between moisture and surface texture, so I don't recommend it for quick-cooking techniques that revolve around browning or a crispy skin. One way to flavor and moisten without sacrificing browning is to marinate in salted oil, which promotes crisping and browning, since the surface of the meat will be infused with oil rather than water. This is especially useful for small pieces of meat, for which you want to maximize browning.

Tempering: Leave meat at room temperature for at least an hour before cooking. With red meat, it's fine to temper it for up to four hours. Cooking tempered meat (as opposed to cold, refrigerated meat) reduces the absolute temperature change the meat will undergo, thus reducing moisture loss.

Also, according to Harold McGee,[1] the longer a steak spends tempering, the more enzymatic (read: flavor-improving) reactions take place. Feel free to temper your steak somewhere warm.

Cooking: Executed properly, searing maximizes flavor by creating a heavily browned crust on the outside of the meat. Render some of your meat's fat to oil the pan. I insist. You might as well stop reading if you're already skipping an easy step that makes food taste better. Some chefs would argue that they prefer searing with olive oil, because it affords a "cleaner" flavor profile. *Pffff.* You can pick your spots for refinement, and seared meat is not the spot. Seriously, when have you ever complained that beef was too beefy or chicken was too chicken-y? That's nonsense, and it would be nonsense to ignore this simple rule of meat cookery. The only time I would not use animal fat is when the meat will be served cold, like in a rare-beef salad, since the residual fat will congeal. Otherwise, cooking the meat in its own fat is the way to go. Trim some fat off and throw it in the pan on medium heat to render, remove the spent chunks, and then raise the temperature to sear the meat. The hotter the better, so you can brown the meat quickly, before proceeding to more gentle heat to finish cooking. Disable the smoke alarm if necessary.

---

1 Harold McGee, *On Food and Cooking: The Science and Lore of the Kitchen* (New York: Scribner, 2004), 143–144.

You can use a probe thermometer to gauge the internal temperature of meat, but bear in mind that the internal temperature will continue rising after you remove the meat from the pan. If you want medium-rare steak, go ahead and pull it before it hits 130°F; the internal temperature will keep climbing for a few minutes and degrees. But it's also easy enough to determine the progress of your steak by pressing it with your fingers, which is fast and enables you to cook meat properly without the crutch of gadgetry. There are all sorts of little tricks to feeling for doneness, and I'll try to give you some guidelines, but the only way to really figure it out is by touching your own meat (ha). Going from raw to rare involves raising the internal temperature from about 70°F–80°F (if it's properly tempered) to 120°F. If your steak feels pretty "bouncy," it's still rare, but things are more nuanced as you go from rare to medium rare, because we're only talking about a temperature range of 10 degrees or so. If a steak has a slight give, residual heat will probably take it to a perfect medium-rare. If it feels firm, and juice is leaching out of the top a bit, you're looking at a medium steak. If you accidentally leave the steak in the pan beyond this point, then it's medium-well. If you keep cooking after that, well, God help you.

Resting: Unless you like dry meat sitting in a puddle of blood, don't start slicing immediately after cooking. Your steak will con-

tinue to cook as heat redistributes through the meat, resulting in better juice retention (a process that professional cooks refer to as "riding out"). Resting for ten minutes per inch of thickness is a reasonable rule of thumb, or, in the case of a whole chicken or turkey, keeping it in a warm place for 4–5 minutes per pound up to 5 pounds, and then 3–4 minutes per pound thereafter.

Steak

Ribeye is my favorite cut of beef. It's fatty and tastes beefy in a slightly gamey way. Plus, in my opinion (and Jeffrey Steingarten's, too), the best part of the entire cow is on the ribeye (see *figure 1*).[2] The *Spinalis dorsi*—also called the lifter or the rib cap—is the narrow strip of super marbled meat on the other side of the "rib's-eye" from the bone. Always choose the ribeye with the biggest lifter.

Portioning your steaks: Whenever possible, I steer away from pre-cut steaks in favor of buying an entire rib roast and breaking it down into steak-like portions that run perpendicular to the cuts we usually find at the butcher shop or the supermarket (*see figure 2*). Cutting portions this way might seem counterintuitive, but there are two reasons to butcher your steaks in this direction, and they both involve the grain of the meat. For

---

2 "Most butchers do not know the words *Spinalis dorsi* though they acknowledge this strip to be the most flavorful and juicy beef you can think of." Jeffrey Steingarten, *It Must've Been Something I Ate* (New York: Alfred A. Knopf, 2002), 453.

FIGURE 1: THE LIFTER

LIFTER

A narrow strip of heavily marbled, tender meat on the ribeye.

NOT THE LIFTER

The grain is tighter and less fatty on the rest of the ribeye.

FIGURE 2: PORTIONING A RIB ROAST

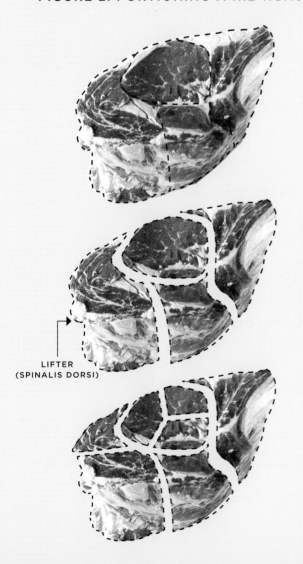

LIFTER
(SPINALIS DORSI)

FIGURE 3: MEAT STRAWS, AND CUTTING ACROSS THE GRAIN

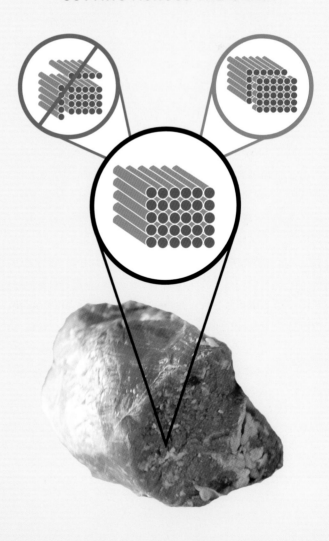

explanatory purposes, it might be useful to imagine the fibers of meat as a bundle of drinking straws. If you sawed through a bundle of straws along the grain, parallel to the straws, then you'd just have a few intact straws; if you cut through it against the grain, perpendicular to the straws, then you have a bunch of tiny straw cross-sections (*see Figure 3, previous page*). Meat fibers are quite different from drinking straws (that is, until 2013, when MSF will go live with my patented "Meat Straws"), but perhaps the comparison can illustrate how chewing on a loose network of short meat fibers is preferable to chewing through longer strands of meat. Portioning your own steak is the best way to ensure that when you slice the cooked meat, the knife will be cutting across the grain.

The other reason to portion your steak this way involves the effect of grain on cooking performance. Going back to the drinking-straws analogy, there is moisture inside and around the fibers. When heat is applied, the fibers contract, and the juice starts to release and evaporate. If the fibers are cooked vertically, the moisture flows right out, but if the fibers are long and cooked horizontally, less juice is lost from within and around each fiber. Of course, the process is not as drastic as liquid flowing out of a straw, but when it comes to a juicy steak, every bit counts.

The typical method of steak butchery probably makes sense from the perspective of the supermarket, trying to sell meat in easily recognizable shapes and in fewer categories—the same reasons we moved away from heirloom varietals in favor of uniform-looking but bland tomatoes. But the classic American ribeye cut is not ideal, in spite of its popularity. And my preference for butchering against the grain applies to other cuts of meat, too. In Argentina—the beef capital of the world—you never see the iconic medallion of filet mignon, because they butcher tenderloins for proper against-the-grain slicing. This is just another one of those things, like the metric system, where people in the rest of the world know what's up.

And as long as we're dissecting the conventions of American butchery, I'd like to submit a modest proposal: steaks should be portioned according to the desired degree of doneness. If you like your meat rare, don't buy a $1/4$" steak and expect to get any browning. And if you try to cook a two-inch-thick steak to medium, then by the time the middle is pink and juicy, a wide margin on each side will be gray and overcooked. Instead, we should be buying or portioning steaks with an eye on the endgame. If you're shooting for medium, portion steaks 1" thick; if you're shooting for medium-rare, portion your rib roast into steaks that are $1^{1}/_{4}$" thick—making for the ideal ratio of crusty exterior to tender interior. The obsession with thick steaks is like the obsession with breast size—it can be a tantalizing distraction from the bigger picture. It's all about proportion, people.

RIBEYE

MAKES 4 LARGE SERVINGS | APPROXIMATE COST: $25–$60

I'm sympathetic to food ethics, and I try to buy responsible products, but you have to pick your battles. I usually buy mid-range meat, like Angus ribeye, especially when it goes on sale for five dollars per pound. You can apply the same techniques to really expensive and responsible steak, too. (But you might want to check with your physical trainer and nutritionist about the gratuitous use of beef fat.)

YOU WILL NEED:

ONE 5–7 POUND RIB ROAST WITH A LARGE "LIFTER" (SEE PAGE 122)

KOSHER SALT

1. Portion steaks (see page 122).

3. On the day you're cooking, temper steaks for at least 30 minutes and up to 4 hours.

2. Salt and age steaks for 2 days, using about 1 tablespoon of salt per pound.

Everything you're doing is intended to strike the ideal balance between hard caramelization on the outside and gentle cooking inside. Keep in mind that a thoroughly tempered steak cooks quickly. For me, major-league caramelization is worth a ring of well-done flesh along the exterior.

4. Render fat removed during butchering/portioning.

5. Sear steaks for one minute on each side in $1/8$" of smoking hot beef fat.

You want enough fat to penetrate the surface irregularities, but not enough to shallow fry. Sear until you have a really nice crust on the exterior. The interior will still be basically raw/rare.

6. Remove steaks from the pan.

Don't overcrowd your pan. Only sear one or two steaks at a time. "Hold" the seared steaks in a warm place, ideally at 100°F–120°F. Allow the fat to cool down significantly. When you're ready to serve, you can either put the steaks in a 250°F oven, or baste them with hot fat to finish. Basting further browns the surface and gives you a sense of accomplishment.

7. If you're finishing the steaks by basting them, tip the pan toward you, place the steak on the far end, and repeatedly spoon hot fat on top of the meat. Welcome to fine dining.

8. Once the steak has reached the desired degree of doneness, remove and rest it in a warmish place for another 7–10 minutes. Most cooks would rather slice their own wrists than an unrested piece of meat. In the words of C+C Music Factory, "chill baby baby chill baby baby wait."

RARE BEEF TOSTADA

MAKES 6 SERVINGS | APPROXIMATE COST: $16

I'd like to regale you with a tale about my recent getaway to a quaint but sophisticated mountain hamlet, where I encountered this local favorite, but I've actually never even been to the French–Mexican border. Still, I really enjoy the combination of seared, rare steak and capers. In addition to complementing this steak-tartare hybrid, caper aioli is a good update to tartar sauce that pairs well with fish, chicken, or potatoes. You can punch up this recipe with some finely cut scallions, shallots, or hot peppers. *C'est parfait pour une soirée de Cinco de Mayo or es perfecto para la fiesta del Bastille Day.*

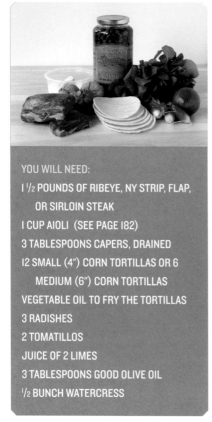

YOU WILL NEED:

1 ½ POUNDS OF RIBEYE, NY STRIP, FLAP,
   OR SIRLOIN STEAK

1 CUP AIOLI (SEE PAGE 182)

3 TABLESPOONS CAPERS, DRAINED

12 SMALL (4") CORN TORTILLAS OR 6
   MEDIUM (6") CORN TORTILLAS

VEGETABLE OIL TO FRY THE TORTILLAS

3 RADISHES

2 TOMATILLOS

JUICE OF 2 LIMES

3 TABLESPOONS GOOD OLIVE OIL

½ BUNCH WATERCRESS

1. Salt the steak 1–3 days in advance (see page 120).

If you've just made fresh aioli (see page 182) you can just toss the capers into the food processor for a few seconds with the finished aioli. Capers are sold either packed in salt or in brine. Depending on your tolerance for salt, you may want to rinse and/or soak the capers to de-salinate.

2. Mince the capers and mix them with the aioli.

3. Fry the tortillas whole until crisp. Salt generously while they're still hot and greasy.

4. Temper and sear the steak to rare. Rest it after cooking (see page 122).

5. Thinly shave or slice the radishes, and pick 1"–3" segments of watercress.

6. Dice the tomatillo into ¼" cubes and dice the steak into ¼" to ⅓" cubes.

7. Toss both with lime juice, olive oil, salt, and pepper to taste.

8. Spoon 2 tablespoons of the aioli onto a tortilla and spread it almost to the edges.

9. Top with a large mound of the dressed meat and tomatillo.

10. Lightly dress the watercress and radishes in vinaigrette, and top each tostada with a generous plume of salad. Taste each component before plating, and adjust with a squirt of lime, a splash of oil, and/or a pinch of salt.

Slow Cooking

The standard fine-dining approach to dealing with cheap, tough cuts of meat has always been slow cooking. Modern haute cuisine takes it even further, vacuum-sealing the meat in a bag and cooking it in a water bath at a controlled temperature for hours or even days—this method has come to be called "sous vide" (which is surprising, given that "vacuum hot-tub relaxation" is a much better term). Really fancy places even have ovens with variable humidity and "reverse-delta technology," which consists of a temperature probe in the meat (a.k.a. "the ol' probe-in-the-sauna gag"), linked to a computer that gradually raises the oven temperature ten degrees above the meat's temperature until the meat reaches the target final temperature, resulting in meat cooked as gently as possible. If, like me, you don't have access to an immersion circulator and vacuum sealer or a fancy oven, you can still achieve good results by braising meat slowly in a regular oven, or better yet, a cheap crock pot. Once properly cooked and cooled, a braised protein is ready for the quick reheating required for restaurant service or a simple but luxurious home meal.

The principle behind slow cooking is straightforward: cook meat in such a way that the protein fibers remain moist while the fat, collagen, and connective tissue melt (above 160°F). A reliable way to do this is to braise meat while submerging it in a rich and flavorful liquid, and cooking it at a low temperature. A braise is ready when the meat is yielding and starting to fall apart. You *can* overcook braises—especially leaner cuts—and keep in mind that the meat will continue to cook in the hot liquid even after you pull it from the oven or turn off the slow cooker. But if you're working with a fatty cut like pork belly, there's a lot of room for error.

You can also let a braising meat "ride out" for a long time, or even overnight. A closed oven stays warm enough to prevent bacterial growth for many hours—"reverse-reverse-delta technology," if you will.

Proper cooling is crucial when you're braising. Plan ahead so you have enough time to cool the meat thoroughly, preferably for a few hours at room temperature, then in the refrigerator overnight. As the braised meat cools, it reabsorbs a lot of liquid, yielding a succulent finished product. If you don't have time or space to cool the entire braise thoroughly, you can wait until the meat is cool enough to handle, pull it out of the hot liquid, and wrap it completely in plastic to cool. Danny Bowien employs this approach at Mission Chinese Food, allowing us to complete numerous braises with an extremely limited amount of time, oven space, storage space, and braising liquid.

Once the braise has completely cooled, the meat can be unwrapped or removed from the braising liquid, which might require that you squeegee the gelatinous liquid off with your hands or a soft spatula. At this point, the meat can be portioned, the fat saved, and the braising liquid reduced into a sauce or reserved for future braises. To serve, reheat the portioned meat in the braising liquid or crisp/brown it by deep frying or searing.

If you're braising meat in a relatively mild liquid, flavor it in advance by salting, brining, or marinating. I don't recommend brining meats cooked to temperature, because it will impede searing and browning, but since braises are submerged in liquid, browning is a lower priority. Thus brining remains the best option for flavoring pork, chicken, and other mild meats you might be braising. Food scientists are divided on whether brining causes salt water to enter the meat's cells or fill the spaces around the cells, but regardless, it adds moisture, slightly denatures the meat, and reduces the cooking time a little bit. A basic brine recipe is $1/3$ cup of salt per quart of water, with as much sugar, herbs, and/or spices as you desire. One quart of brine per 2–3 pounds of meat should be sufficient. You can brine overnight in a plastic bag if you don't have an appropriately shaped vessel— just squeeze the air out of the bag to ensure that the meat is submerged.

That said, post-brine browning is better than no browning at all, so dry off your meat when it comes out of the brine, and sear it in a hot pan prior to braising.

You can apply the same principles to plenty of cuts of meat. Again, the main steps are 1) flavoring, 2) browning, 3) slowly cooking in flavorful liquid, 4) cooling, 5) portion-ing, 6) reheating to serve. With leaner cuts of meat, you'll get a better result with a richer braising liquid and a lower cooking temperature, like a 250°F oven or a slow cooker.

It's simple, really: just two days of your life and you're ready for a quick and easy one-pot meal.

Pork Belly

I learned how to make pork belly from Jason Fox. Everybody's cooking pork belly these days, but everyone's also using heirloom tomatoes when they're in season—no need to overthink things that are irresistibly delicious. I deviate from conventional braising liquids like chicken stock and white wine in favor of the Chinese method of employing a "master sauce"—a fortified stock achieved by reusing the same sauce over and over. Some Western cooks find this gross, but to me, wasting perfectly good meaty broth is gross. The concentrated braising liquid results in a richer flavor, so if you've got it, flaunt it.

My personal preference for this dates back to cooking as a teenager, when we'd make ribs in barbecue sauce and re-use the sauce for a second generation of ribs, then a third. Eventually we'd have a "seventh-gen" sauce, which tasted really "porky" and "awesome." Don't strain the fat off your master stock/sauce. When it cools, the fat will congeal on top and form a natural airtight seal. If you bring it to a boil and then cool it periodically, it should keep indefinitely—especially since it is high in salt.

The DENIM DIET

KAM■ GRAY

16 SIMPLE HABITS to Get You Into Your Dream Pair of Jeans

Skinny Bitch

PORK BELLY

MAKES 16 SERVINGS | APPROXIMATE COST: $25

Around 2005, a unilateral decree was handed down ordering every restaurant in the country to start serving pork belly. MSF was certainly not immune to the charms of this hallowed cut of meat, even if it's played out. There are a lot of ways to cook it, but if, like me, you enjoy eating things that are crispy on the outside and soft on the inside, you're in luck. This recipe yields a thoroughly browned, crunchy exterior, as well as a gush of liquid pork fat when you bite into it.

YOU WILL NEED:
8-LB PORK BELLY SIDE (SKIN OPTIONAL)
2 QUARTS WATER
²/₃ CUP KOSHER SALT
¹/₂ CUP SUGAR
BRINING SPICES OF YOUR CHOICE

1. Score the fat side of the belly with ¹/₈"–deep slashes every ¹/₂".

2. Repeat in the opposite direction, to form a grid pattern.

3. Cut slabs of pork belly that will fit in your biggest frying pan.

4. Combine the salt, sugar, spices, and water to make a brine.

For MSF pork belly, I used a brine composed of 2 quarts water, ²/₃ cups of salt, ¹/₂ cup of sugar, and a handful of fennel seeds, star anise, coriander, black pepper, and bay leaf. You could also play around with thyme, cumin, juniper, and mustard. If you have the time, toast the spices before putting them in the brine.

The brine proportions in this recipe should vary, depending on the salinity of your braising liquid. If you're using plain chicken stock and some wine, then you may want more salt in the brine. If you're using a flavorful master stock, you can almost skip the brine altogether, perhaps just sprinkling salt on the pork belly an hour in advance.

5. Submerge bellies in brine, and weigh them down with plates. Refrigerate overnight.

6. Remove bellies from brine and pat dry. Heat a big nonstick or stainless-steel pan.

7. Sear the bellies in ⅛" to ¼" of pork fat to ensure even browning.

Use enough fat to penetrate the scored crevices. There's little danger of overcooking, since the meat is super fatty. Start with the fat side down, because it's less prone to sticking. Carefully lower it into the pan. It will sizzle and pop like crazy, and probably burn you even if you're cautious. Sorry.

8. Once the fat side is browned, flip and brown the meaty side for 2–4 minutes.

Searing renders some of the fat and raises the overall level of umami. If you're in a real time crunch, you could skip the searing, but you could also just skip lunch and spend the time searing your pork belly properly. It's all about priorities.

If you want to speed things up, heat your braising liquid separately while you're searing the pork.

9. Place meat in a roasting pan large enough to hold it all, and cover with braising liquid.

10. Cover with parchment and then two layers of foil. Place in a 300°F oven.

Without the parchment, the foil might stick to your meat when the fatty bellies float upward. The second piece of foil makes for a better seal around the edges since the foil crushes onto itself, providing more of a purchase than the smooth hard edge of your roasting vessel. Depending on how thick your belly is, it can braise in the oven for 4–6 hours at 280°F–300°F.

11. Pork belly is hard to overcook, so use a higher temp if you absolutely need to. The bellies are done when the meat is shreddable and the fat is melty and easily smashed with tongs. Cool overnight, then squeegee the braising liquid off the bellies back into the pan before portioning.

12. Portion into 1 1/4" to 1 1/2" squares (bigger for the thinner parts of the belly).

13. We deep-fry the chunks to reheat. But portion and reheat them however you like.

Serve on buttery flatbreads (see page 169), with pickled jicama (see below), cilantro aioli, and pickled jalapeño (see below). Reserve the braising liquid for sauce or freeze for a future braise. You can also reduce the liquid for the sake of freezer space and then just add water as needed later.

=== ACCOMPANIMENTS ===

MARINATED JICAMA & PICKLED JALAPEÑO

MAKES 16 SERVINGS
APPROXIMATE COST: $3 FOR JICAMA, $5 FOR JALAPEÑO

FOR THE JICAMA, YOU WILL NEED:
1 LARGE JICAMA
3 TABLESPOONS LIME JUICE
4 TEASPOONS FISH SAUCE
PINCH OF SUGAR

FOR THE JALAPEÑOS, YOU WILL NEED:
1 POUND RED JALAPEÑOS
1 1/2 CUPS LIGHT-COLORED VINEGAR
1 CUP WATER
1/2 CUP SUGAR

1. Slice the skin off the exterior of the jicama.

2. Cut jicama into 1/4" slices, then 1/4" batons. Combine with other jicama ingredients.

3. Refrigerate in a plastic bag for at least 30 minutes, or as long as overnight.

1. Slice jalapeños into 1/8"-thick coins.

2. Combine vinegar, water, and sugar. Bring to a boil.

3. Remove from heat. Pour over jalapeños, and allow to cool thoroughly.

BRAISED SAUSAGE

MAKES 8 SERVINGS | APPROXIMATE COST: $14

Braised sausage is a luxurious and uncomplicated dish, but is surprisingly uncommon on the West Coast. You sacrifice the snap of a seared casing and the juiciness of simply grilled sausage—but hey, you don't eat potato dauphinoise for the rustic roasted-potato experience. If you want to gussy this dish up a bit, braise or slow-cook sauerkraut in the same vessel. The sauerkraut will absorb fat and flavorful liquid, becoming very tasty, but will no longer be bright, crisp, and sour. This is also a nice time to break out the slow cooker, in which case you can let it go on low overnight.

YOU WILL NEED:

8 UNCOOKED SAUSAGES OF ANY KIND
    (I PREFER A NEUTRAL VARIETY, LIKE
    BRATWURST)
3 ONIONS, SLICED THIN
I CUP STOCK, CIDER, OR WATER
I BOTTLE OF BEER
2 CUPS SAUERKRAUT, DRAINED OVER A
    COLANDER (OPTIONAL)

I. Brown the sausages in a pan with some animal fat or oil.

2. Place the browned sausages in a deep ovenproof pan or in a slow-cooker pot.

3. Brown the onions briefly, then add them to the pan with the browned sausages.

4. Optional: heat sauerkraut in a pan, and add on top of the onions and sausages.

5. Add a combination of stock/wine/cider/water/beer to just cover the contents.

6. Cover with a layer of parchment and two layers of foil.

7. Braise at 300°F for a few hours, until the sausage is extremely soft.

MISSION BURGER

(Above) Danny, Momma, and Tony the Butcher.

(Below) A relatively long example of the granulated burger meat column.

Mission Burger

For a few months, Mission Street Food served technique-driven burgers from the deli counter of an Asian supermarket up the block.

Our method for the patties was originally conceived by one of the world's most respected chefs and one of my personal heroes, Heston Blumenthal. In his TV-and-book series *In Search of Perfection*, Blumenthal dissects conventional dishes and then outlines a methodology for creating his ideal version. We admired Blumenthal's hamburger technique and dubbed his process "granulation," since it organized the burger into

a pattern resembling the grain of a steak. Granulation provides an elegant solution to a common problem facing most burgers: overly dense patties. Organizing the meat strands and slicing patties with a knife results in a relatively smooth-faced yet uncompressed patty, which in turn allows a cook to sear the outside extremely hard without sacrificing tenderness or moisture.

From Blumenthal's baseline, we tried to enhance the flavors by applying the principles that guide our approach to steaks. That is, we aged the meat for two to three days before grinding, and we seared the meat in rendered beef fat.

Mission Burgers really represent the pinnacle of the MSF style, which applies haute-cuisine technique to food with a broad appeal. Granulation elevates the burger without adding truffles, foie gras, or bacon, and it stands in direct contrast to "burgers of privilege" made from bovine aristocracy. We sold Mission Burgers for $8 each, and donated a buck from each burger to the local food bank. If you decide to follow this blueprint at a burger joint of your own, I wish you all the success in the world, but the charitable donation is a crucial step in the whole labor-intensive-but-rewarding process, and you should not skip it any more than you should skip the granulation. Use some decent buns, too, while you're at it. We served our burgers with a homemade caper aioli and grilled onions.

MISSION BURGER

MAKES 16 BURGERS | APPROXIMATE COST: $45

Only an ambitious home cook will go the whole nine yards and make something as complex as a granulated burger, but this recipe illustrates a larger point about effort and technique. There's no reason something should be cooked a certain way just because that's the way it's usually done. When I think back on all those burgers I formed by hand, slapping ground beef thoughtlessly back and forth, back and forth, I weep with shame. Then I brine pork belly in those hot, bitter tears. (*Note: The photos below depict the production of about sixty burgers.*)

FOR THE PATTIES, YOU WILL NEED:
4 1/2 POUNDS OF CHUCK
2 1/2 POUNDS OF BRISKET
3 POUNDS OF SHORT RIB
1-2 POUNDS BEEF FAT, DEPENDING ON
   HOW FATTY YOUR MEAT IS
AT LEAST 1/2 CUP OF KOSHER SALT
PLASTIC WRAP (THE WIDER, THE BETTER)

FOR THE TOPPINGS, YOU WILL NEED:
RENDERED BEEF FAT
4 ONIONS
16 SLICES MONTEREY JACK CHEESE
3 CUPS CAPER AIOLI (SEE PAGE 128)
16 MEDIUM-SIZED BUNS, OR ENGLISH
   MUFFINS

1. Using a sharp knife, remove "silver skin" and tough, gristly parts from each cut of meat and reserve for making stock.

2. Trim off large pieces of fat and reserve. Some fat may remain on the meat.

3. Cut meat into 1" cubes, keeping them separated.

After all the trimming is done, you should end up with roughly 7 pounds of trimmed meat, for which you'll need about 1 1/2 pounds of fat (the desired ratio is 4 parts meat to 1 part fat).

In the next step, you'll need a 1/2 cup of salt for 7 pounds of meat (just under a tablespoon of kosher salt per pound of meat.)

4. Salt the meat and spread it onto racks. Refrigerate uncovered for two days.

5. Cut the fat into ½″ cubes.

6. Weigh the total amount of beef, keeping the chuck separate from brisket and short rib.

7. Grind the fat with the brisket and short rib. (See note on proportions after step 3.)

8. Make a wide landing strip of plastic wrap, using multiple, overlapping layers.

9. Grind the mixture again, this time adding the chuck to create textural variation.

10. As the meat strands emerge from the grinder, carefully collate them by laying them on plastic wrap in a parallel formation. Stack the strands to create a pile with a 5″ girth.

11. Bundle the strands with the plastic wrap, to form a "meat column."

12. Press firmly so the column holds together, but don't compress it too much.

13. Slice the column with a sharp knife to form patties that are ³/₄" to 1" thick.

14. Sear onions in very hot beef fat until mostly soft. They'll finish cooking on their own.

15. Sear each patty in beef fat over high heat for 60–90 seconds, until a crust forms.

Never grill this kind of patty, because all of the fat and moisture will drip right out (a prime example of the "drinking straws analogy"—see page 124). Searing in a generous amount of fat creates an all-important moisture-sealing crust.

16. As the burger cooks, cut the tops off the buns and toast. Top one half with cheese.

17. Flip the patty carefully, and sear the other side for 45–60 seconds. Transfer the patty to an ungreased pan over medium heat to finish cooking, and to allow some grease to drain off.

18. Top the patty with onions and cheesy bun.

19. Rest in a warm spot for another 2 minutes to finish cooking/draining.

20. Smear 1 ½ tablespoons of caper aioli on the bottom bun, and assemble burgers.

Peking Duck

I've spent a month eating my way around China, but my favorite Peking duck is in an old strip mall in the suburbs of Washington, DC at Peking Gourmet Inn. The walls are chockablock with pictures of politicians and celebrities, all smiling the same Peking duck–induced smile. Ducks are carved table-side by lifelong professionals who expertly unfurl broad swaths of crispy skin and slices of tender meat. The restaurant owners serve the duck with a special variety of yellow spring onion grown on their own farm, along with hoisin sauce, soy-cured peppers, juli-enned cucumber, and (crucially) thin flour wrappers. The entire ensemble is sublimely satisfying; it's a dish I could eat every day.

The traditional preparation of Peking duck involves separating the skin from the fat with a kind of bellows. (Some friends tried to simulate this with a bike pump before resorting to the air compressor at the gas station.) The ducks are then air-dried for one to two days to remove excess water from the skin, then roasted by hanging over wood embers in a brick oven, so the fat can render and the duck can self-baste.

Unfortunately, this was not even remotely possible in the small refrigera-tors and half-broken oven at Mission Street Food. However, it's the crispy skin, hoisin, and cucumber combo that really brings the dish home for me, so it's still possible to approach that Peking-duck epiphany with-out doing anything the right way. We served variations of this flavor combo in tacos, flatbread sandwiches, and even something we called a Chinito (a rice noodle wrapped around a Chinese donut stuffed with the usual suspects).

PEKING DUCK

MAKES 6 SERVINGS | APPROXIMATE COST: $20-35, DEPENDING ON WHETHER YOU USE CHICKEN OR DUCK

Peking duck is all about the crispy skin. Our alternative to roasting whole ducks is to start with separate skins and make cracklin. Ideally, you'd use duck skin, but chicken skin is easier to obtain and is a more than acceptable substitution. Your local butcher might be nice enough to just give you their unwanted poultry skins, but act quickly—chicken skin is the new bacon, and soon opportunists will be selling novelties like chicken wrapped in chicken skin.

YOU WILL NEED:

I POUND RAW DUCK SKINS

9 CONFITED DUCK OR CHICKEN LEG
    QUARTERS (SEE SIDEBAR ON
    NEXT PAGE)

2 CUPS HOISIN SAUCE

5-10 THAI CHILIES

CUCUMBER, SCALLION, AND CILANTRO
    FOR GARNISH

12 SCALLION PANCAKES, TORTILLAS, OR
    FLATBREADS (SEE PAGE 169)

1. Salt the skins and lay them on a tray in a single layer between pieces of parchment.

3. Bake for 45 minutes at 300°F, or until there are no soft, fatty parts.

4. The skins will crisp up once they cool down. Set aside, and try not to eat them.

2. Cover with another sheet tray to keep the skins flat.

This is a good place to start your collection of chicken or duck fat. Pour off the fat from the sheet tray before it congeals, and reserve it. Don't be shy about wringing fat out of the parchment.

5. Separate the confit quarters into skin, meat, and bones.

You can fry the skins from your duck or chicken confit and supplement your cracklins, giving you both disc-shaped skin chips and crispy curls.

6. Blend chilies and I cup of the hoisin sauce. Don't blend all of the hoisin.

7. Fold the chili-hoisin purée into the rest of the hoisin sauce.

8. Fry the tortillas, flatbreads, or pancakes in duck or chicken fat.

You can make simple traditional wrappers by combining 2 cups of flour, 2 ounces of lard, and I $^3/_4$ cups of hot water, resting it, portioning it, and rolling out thin discs. Fry those in a non-stick pan. (More experienced Peking duck geeks have made detailed recipes for these wrappers readily available online.)

9. Gather breads, duck meat, crispy skins, hoisin, and garnishes.

The main idea here is that Peking duck does not need to be some ossified tradition enshrined on a brick oven and wood-ember pedestal. Any version of Peking duck is better than pretty much anything else.

ACCOMPANIMENT

DUCK OR CHICKEN CONFIT

MAKES 6 SERVINGS | APPROXIMATE COST: $25 ($12 IF USING CHICKEN)

Duck fat adds a lot of flavor, but is more expensive and harder to come by than chicken fat. Feel free to substitute chicken fat or chicken meat, based on cost or availability.

YOU WILL NEED:
9 DUCK LEG QUARTERS OR CHICKEN LEG QUARTERS
2 QUARTS RENDERED DUCK OR CHICKEN FAT

I. Salt poultry generously and refrigerate overnight. Cover with fat.

2. Cover with parchment and two layers of foil. Cook in a 300°F oven for 3 hours.

3. The meat should be very tender. Cool before picking, so the meat remains moist.

HAM HOCK RILLETTE

MAKES 6 ENTREE SERVINGS | APPROXIMATE COST: $18

A rillette is shredded meat moistened with fat and liquid. The texture of rillette ranges from pâté to tuna salad to pulled pork. It's extremely versatile—it can adorn a charcuterie plate or a salad, it can be folded into pasta, it can elevate hot or cold sandwiches. Rillette is often made with pork or duck, but any slow-cooked meat may be subject to rillettification. I like to use ham hocks because they furnish three valuable qualities in one inexpensive meat-bundle: smokiness, sumptuousness, and gelatinousness (for more on gelatin purées, *see page 194*).

YOU WILL NEED:

5 POUNDS MEATY HAM HOCKS

3 QUARTS CHICKEN STOCK, PORK
    STOCK, DASHI, OR WATER

2 CUPS BACON FAT OR PORK FAT

SALT, SHERRY VINEGAR, MUSTARD,
    SPICES, FRESH HERBS, AND/OR
    GARLIC TO TASTE

1. Gently simmer ham hocks in chicken
   stock, pork stock, dashi, or water.

3. Cool the entire pot until you can handle
   the hocks. Drain and reserve the stock.

2. After about 4 hours, the meat should be
   very tender.

4. At the end, you'll have plenty of stock left
   for cooking greens, or just for sipping.

5. Pick the ham hocks apart by hand.

6. Separate the meat from the skins and
   soft collagen. Reserve both.

The edges of ham hocks can become
dried out and tough from the
smoking process or from not being
fully submerged in liquid. Move the
hocks around periodically as they
simmer, and discard any parts that may
be too tough to rillette.

Discard any tough skin, bones,
and weird gristle.

7. Blend the skins with just enough stock to get the mix going, creating a gelatin purée.

8. Strain the purée through a fine sieve, using a ladle or spoon to push it through.

9. Combine the meat, and some of the purée, fat, vinegar, and spices in a stand mixer.

10. Mix using the medium-low setting and the paddle attachment of your mixer.

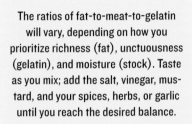

The ratios of fat-to-meat-to-gelatin will vary, depending on how you prioritize richness (fat), unctuousness (gelatin), and moisture (stock). Taste as you mix; add the salt, vinegar, mustard, and your spices, herbs, or garlic until you reach the desired balance.

11. For best results, mix the rillette at the temperature it will be served.

12. In addition to ham-hock stock, there'll be lots of leftover gelatin purée, which you can use to enrich anything from meatballs to gravy. If you're not quite ready to jump into another meat-centric project, it's okay to freeze the purée for later use.

CHICKEN WINGS

MAKES 6 SERVINGS | APPROXIMATE COST: $20

The middle segment of a chicken wing has an ideal ratio and juxtaposition of skin to meat, and they're about as cheap as whole wings. You can cook the heck out of them, because the meat is close to the bone and the whole thing is protected by skin. In fact, we cook them three times, achieving the kind of papery crisp skin that once had Michael Pollan eating out of the palms of our hands. (This really happened! Sort of. Long story.) As an added bonus, you can store par-fried, frozen wings for weeks, leaving you always ready to host an impromptu *Biggest Loser* marathon.

YOU WILL NEED:

4 POUNDS CHICKEN-WING MIDDLE SEGMENTS, SALTED LIBERALLY AND REFRIGERATED OVERNIGHT ON A RACK (OR IN A BOWL, IF YOU DON'T HAVE ROOM)

OIL FOR FRYING

SALT AND WHATEVER SEASONINGS YOU WANT (TRY CAYENNE, OR, IF YOU WANT TO BE CULTURALLY DIVERSE, ZA'ATAR)

Note: This is a whole chicken wing, cut to reveal the middle segment.

2. Freeze the wings for at least 2 hours.

I. Fry the wings at 280°F for 6 minutes.

It's okay to buy frozen wings. Freezing bursts cell walls in the skin, so that more water can evaporate during subsequent frying sessions. Freezing after each frying also prevents the meat from getting overcooked.

4. Par-fry the frozen wings again for 6 minutes at 280°F. Freeze again.

5. To serve, fry the wings at 350°F–375°F for about 5 minutes, or until crispy.

Season with salt and whatever spices you desire, but don't add sauce! If you have an allegiance to Buffalo wings or a fish-sauce glaze, serve it as a dipping sauce, but don't ruin your crispy little masterpieces by soaking them in wetness. You're ready to open the best wing shop in the country—just make sure you have no social life, because your days will be consumed by an endless cycle of par-frying and freezing.

SEAFOOD

Fish

If you'd asked me three years ago how to cook fish, I would have suggested a hard pan-fry, in pursuit of perfectly crisp skin. But after a few years in fine dining and experimenting at MSF, I've decided that there are bigger fish to fry, metaphorically speaking. You just can't achieve crisp skin without sacrificing the delicate texture of the flesh, and the flesh is a higher priority. (If, like me, you have an untreatable skin condition, you can simply remove the fish skin beforehand and crisp it separately (*see page 80*). To achieve a shatteringly crispy skin chip, salt, bake at a low temperature until the skin is dry, then fry. You can also import crispiness from a variety of accompaniments like potato chips, artichoke chips, prosciutto chips, or "chips," as they say across the pond, to name a few.)

Gentle cooking is ideal for most fish, and poaching is my first choice, with steaming close behind. Even a fatty fish like black cod, which remains moist when cooked rigorously, is much more refined when cooked gently. Fish proteins cook rapidly and at such a low temperature that you could poach a piece of fish in a soda can held over a candle. And cooking fish is fundamentally different from cooking meat insofar as you want to showcase the natural grain of the flesh. Piscine musculature is composed of soft, smooth tiles that are pleasing to the tongue, so the goal with most fish is to gently cook the flesh so that it flakes apart, but remains as moist as possible.

Poach your fillets in oil, or a flavored mixture like buttery miso soup or scallion broth, or plain salted water. The temperature should be well below a boil, but above 140°F. If you're dealing with thinner fillets, you can even cook them gently by basting with warm liquid—but not too warm. To avoid inadvertently ruining your fish, you can warm up your liquid in a pan, then turn off the heat before adding and basting your fish. If you're steaming, you can preserve the fish's internal moisture by plastic-wrapping it to a plate or using a Ziploc bag—a.k.a. the poor man's sous vide.[3]

Given the variety of fish, there are obvious exceptions to the rule of gentle fish cookery:

- Small fish like sardines are fatty and mostly prized for their fishy flavor. Sear or fry.

- Catfish flesh has so little structural integrity that it is still soft when cooked to well-done. Fry away.

- Some fish, like tuna, are delicious rare. A hard sear is fine, since you're not even

3 Ziploc actually makes a "Sous Vide" line of bags with one-way valves and a goofy bike-pump contraption. At Bar Tartine, we had another ghetto version of a sous-vide machine: Jason Fox sucking the air out of Ziploc-bagged items with a straw.

cooking the inside. Start with fillets that are $^3/_4$" or thicker.

- Curing fish in salt or acid amounts to "cooking" the flesh. Avoid overcooking.

- I like sushi.

Batter-frying fish is basically equivalent to steaming inside of a crust, so it's not really an exception. Let's call it "gentile cooking." The ideal batter is light and crispy. Heston Blumenthal recommends aerating batter with a whipped-cream charger and replacing some of the water with vodka. The air bubbles keep it light, and the alcohol evaporates faster than water, resulting in a crispier crust. Taking Blumenthal's idea one step too far (as is my wont), you can create an ultra-crisp crust by using 100 percent vodka. If you're going to that extreme, start by coating your fish in a regular batter so that the stuff near the flesh (where liquid doesn't fully evaporate) won't taste like a martini. When Danny and I "hyper-Blumenthaled" at Mission Burger, we also had fun whacking the finished product with a 2" × 4" in admiration of the crisp shell.

Bivalves

It's strange that restaurants charge a lot for mussels. While they're delicious, they're also easy to prepare. If we were ever strapped for time at MSF, mussels were no-brainers, figuratively as well as literally. In fact, if you see mussels served in a res-taurant, you know the chef is taking it easy. That said, if I see green-lipped mussels on a menu, I'll order them. And *that said*, if I see a woman's vagina rimmed with green lipstick, I'll ask for the check.

You can clean mussels, clams, and oysters by placing them under water and vigorously jostling them with your hands to remove exterior dirt. Drain off dirty water as needed. With the seafood fully submerged, leave under a trickle of running water for 10 or 15 minutes. The running water encourages the bivalves to "purge," or expel sand from inside the shell. Debeard mussels and cook until the moment their shells start to open; at MSF, we steamed mussels in a flavorful cooking liquid like curry or buttery broth.

Danny Bowien taught me that clams should be served steamed or boiled until barely cooked—it's okay to stop cooking even before the shells open. You can "unlock" barely opened clams by inserting a butter knife into the slit and slicing the connective muscle holding the shells together. Do this over a bowl to save the delicious clam liquor inside. If you're making clam chowder, set the nicely cooked clams aside, adding them back when serving to avoid overcooking.

I recommend shucking oysters and serving them raw with a complementary accompaniment like cucumber granita or nori powder. I think horseradish, cocktail sauce, Tabasco, mignonette, and even lemon are just distractions from the (theoretically) pristine flavor of the raw oyster.

Shucking an oyster can only be learned through trial and error, but I'll awkwardly describe the basics. First of all, you should get yourself an oyster knife, because you'll hurt yourself if you try to use a regular knife. Wear a thick glove or wrap the oyster in a folded kitchen towel with the cup-like side on the bottom and the pointed hinge-y side toward yourself. Hold it firmly or brace down against a table and insert an oyster knife into that hinge area. Apply some pressure, maybe even a lot of pressure, maneuvering until your oyster knife finds a "foothold," and then twist/pry to pop the top loose. It will still be connected by the oyster's muscles, so at that point, slide/scrape the knife along the flat upper shell to release the oyster from the top, cut-

DANNY'S OCTOPUS A LA PLANCHA

(Above) with smoked yogurt, black olive, young turnips, peas, and ras el hanout.

(Opposite page) The Garby Anka OX-30 Octopus Tenderizer.

ting off as little flesh as possible. Discard the top shell. Scrape the oyster knife along the bottom to release the oyster from the bottom shell—especially around a relatively dense cylindrical fleshy part called the abductor. Run a clean finger along the rim to remove shards of shell or dirt. Tease or flip the oyster with your knife if necessary to improve appearance and check for broken bits of shell. Sniff to ensure freshness; oysters should smell like the ocean, rather than like decay. Don't worry if you're slow at first; once you get the hang of it, you'll get about 5 percent faster every 100 oysters.

Scallops are another no-brainer, all the more so because they're often sold pre-shucked. They're delicious raw or cooked, and have flesh soft enough to sear. I would not even mention them except for their remarkable versatility. You don't need me to tell you what to put with scallops, because pretty much anything works. Just make sure you don't overcook them.

Crustaceans

I'm allergic to crustaceans, so you won't learn anything useful from me on this subject. Let's move on, shall we?

Cephalopods

People should not be weirded out by cephalopods just because they're weird.

Bigfin squid and cuttlefish have a creamy texture when raw, adding a show-stopping element to salads and cold appetizers. You've probably enjoyed fried calamari, but you may not have considered stuffing squid with bone marrow (*see next page*). Squid ink is another intimidating ingredient for the uninitiated, but it adds intense depth of flavor and color to dishes, and it's easier to use than you may think— it's basically a concentrated seafood stock and/or aromatic commercial stain. Don't be discouraged by the $40/lb price tag, because a little goes a long way and the cost works out to be way less than a dollar per serving.

While the prevailing perception is that octopus is rubbery, it's actually satisfyingly toothsome when tenderized and then either cooked quickly just to the point of doneness, or braised slowly. Octopus companies use mechanized octopus tumblers to tenderize the flesh. You can put *your* octopus in a Ziploc bag and use your washing machine's spin cycle, or you can achieve a similar effect by freezing it overnight.

Octopi are highly intelligent—they are capable of opening jars to reach food, and some species camouflage themselves with coconut shells while using their tentacles to walk along the sandy ocean bottom. YouTube it. Scientists now believe they have individual personalities and intellectual capacities analogous to alien intelligence. In the end, all of that just adds a deliciously poignant undertone to mindlessly shoveling them into your gaping maw.

MARROW-STUFFED SQUID

MAKES 4 SERVINGS | **APPROXIMATE COST: $8**

Commonwealth's chef de cuisine Ian Muntzert is a great cook from whom I've learned a lot. We came up with the idea of marrow-stuffed squid in a drunken haze, so we don't know whose idea it was. But when we made it a couple weeks later at MSF, it turned out to be one of the best things I ate that entire year. Ian and Jason serve marrow-stuffed squid at Commonwealth, but their approach is fundamentally different. Their version may be more "refined," but I prefer my marrow big, sloppy, and redolent, like a depth charge of beef, wrapped in a squid torpedo, fired at your gullet.

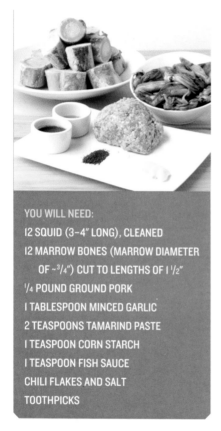

YOU WILL NEED:

12 SQUID (3–4" LONG), CLEANED

12 MARROW BONES (MARROW DIAMETER
    OF ~³/₄") CUT TO LENGTHS OF 1¹/₂"

¹/₄ POUND GROUND PORK

1 TABLESPOON MINCED GARLIC

2 TEASPOONS TAMARIND PASTE

1 TEASPOON CORN STARCH

1 TEASPOON FISH SAUCE

CHILI FLAKES AND SALT

TOOTHPICKS

1. Soak the marrow bones in salty water overnight in the fridge to purge impurities.

3. Roast for 8–10 minutes or until marrow is slightly browned and hot in the center.

2. Preheat the oven to 450°F. Place bones on a baking rack with the flat sides down.

You can test the marrow's doneness by inserting a toothpick, which should then feel warm against your lower lip or wrist.

Once cooked, remove the marrow bones from the pan and allow them to cool to room temperature before working with them. The marrow should be firm.

4. If your squid isn't cleaned, separate the body from tentacles. Remove the beak.

5. Squeeze out the internal organs from the body, and discard them.

6. Pull out the clear cartilage from the body. Discard. Soak cleaned squid in water.

7. Pop the marrow out of the bones with your fingers. Wear latex gloves and work carefully. There are sharp bone spurs inside some femurs.

8. Cut marrow lengthwise into halves or quarters, depending on the size of your squid.

9. Mix pork, garlic, tamarind, corn starch, fish sauce, and chili flakes. Season with salt.

10. Flatten a tablespoon of pork mix in your hand and envelop the marrow in pork.

11. Roll the pork around the marrow to form stubby "torpedoes."

12. Stuff a torpedo into each squid cavity.

13. Sew each squid shut with a toothpick.

14. Salt bodies and tentacles. Sear them on a pan or griddle for 45 seconds on each side.

Squid becomes rubbery when overcooked, so it's important to thoroughly temper the stuffed squid, so that the pork stuffing can cook, and the marrow can become soft and melty before the squid's texture is compromised.

15. Remove the toothpicks and serve with greens and crispy bread shavings as a low-key backdrop for the fireworks of the marrow-and-pork-stuffed squid. Protein trifecta!

VEGETABLES

Vegetables can be the stars of a meal even at the world's best restaurants. There are far too many circumstances and modes of preparation for this section to be exhaustive, so I'll focus on two useful concepts that are part of the canon of classical technique: shocking and glazing.

Many home cooks may wonder how restaurants achieve such vibrant flavor and color in their cooked vegetables: the secret is plunging them in ice water after blanching or steaming. Blanching consists of submerging vegetables in rapidly boiling salty water, which can add flavor and/or leach out bitterness, while steaming retains more of the vegetables' inherent flavor. Choose your method accordingly, but in both cases it's crucial to have plenty of ice water on hand for shocking. Use a strainer or tongs to transfer the cooked vegetables to your ice bath. If you steamed the vegetables, you can salt the ice bath as a way of imparting flavor. Once thoroughly cooled, remove the vegetables from the ice bath to prevent excess water absorption and drain thoroughly, using a salad spinner if necessary. With green vegetables, the combination of rapid cooking and rapid cooling not only preserves the chlorophyll's color, but actually enhances it by forcing out trapped gases. Shocking also ensures that the vegetables don't continue to cook after being removed from the heat.

Glazing is a method of cooking vegetables in a pan with a flavored liquid; in French cooking, this is typically a combination of salt, sugar, butter, and water. I like to add miso for depth. Glazing is especially useful for root vegetables, since the liquid facilitates even cooking. The goal is for the vegetables to cook while liquid evaporates, with the moment of perfect doneness coinciding with total evaporation. It's not actually that tricky; the main idea is to "glaze" the vegetables in their own flavorful juice, which is released during cooking. Start with an educated guess at the amount of water, and add a splash early on if it seems like the rate of evaporation is outpacing the rate of cooking. Conversely, if you're in danger of overcooking but you still have a ton of liquid, strain out the vegetables and remove them from the heat, continue reducing the liquid, and then re-add the vegetables to glaze.

East vs. West

Like most American cooks, I first learned to cook within a Eurocentric culinary tradition. Moving from a Western fine-dining environment to a Chinese take-out joint, I was struck by the sensible yet "foreign" techniques that could—and should—be assimilated into our common culture as cooks. In particular, I want to argue for the value of reuse, which is standard practice in Chinese cooking, the way salting pasta water is standard in Italian cooking.

I mention "master sauces" in the

KING TRUMPET MUSHROOMS
(A.K.A. KING OYSTER)

*Meaty, mild in flavor, and the
centerpiece of MSF's King Trumpet
flatbread sandwich.*

meat section, but Chinese cuisine also centers around reusing oil. Next to every wok in China (that's a lot of woks!) stands a metal container topped with a strainer. Most dishes start with oil from the container and are completed with a quick strain that saves excess oil for later. I was never inclined to cook with a lot of oil, because I didn't want to waste it, but in the reuse paradigm, you're just fortifying your oil with flavor, like a French cook who builds beef broth from chicken broth. You can reuse that oil indefinitely, and though it may not be a good idea to fry apple beignets in oil that's had garlic and mushrooms in it, eggplant fried in that oil has more depth and complexity than it would have otherwise. Used intelligently, oil reuse can improve cooking: every sauté or sear could use flavored oil, and could even be reconsidered as a potential oil poach or shallow-fry.

A QUICK GUIDE TO MUSHROOM PREPARATION

TYPE OF MUSHROOM	PREP FORMAT	COOKING STYLE
Button	Stemmed* and sliced	Raw or gently cooked; unsalted or salted to order
Enoki	Separated into strands or small clusters	
King Trumpet a.k.a. King Oyster	Cut against the grain into coins or semi-circles, maximizing tenderness	Simmer gently submerged in oil; salt generously
Beech a.k.a. Hon Shimeji, Golden Enoki	Stemmed and split into roughly individual stems	Sear on medium high heat in 1/8" oil and leave undisturbed until caramelized; salt generously.
Enoki	Pulled apart into clusters resembling a snack-sized candy bar	
Hen of the woods a.k.a. maitake		
King Trumpet a.k.a. King Oyster	Cut with the grain into pinky-sized batons, maximizing "squidginess"	
Oyster	Stemmed* and cut into 1/2" strips with the grain	
Shiitake	Stemmed* and quartered	

Reserve stems for broth.

Mushrooms are a prime example of how beneficial it can be to deviate from the Eurocentric orientation to oil use, since they're good vehicles for salt and oil (and mysteriously have no calories). In Eastern medicine, mushrooms have myriad health benefits heretofore undiscovered by the West. They also provide depth and umami, and in my opinion, they're the cornerstone of tasty vegetarian food. Though there's a lot of flexibility in terms of preparation, the above chart will outline my default methods of preparation for many common varieties some of which involve a distinctly Eastern amount of oil, even if the mushrooms end up in a Western omelet.[4] Plus, you'll be able to fry your hashbrowns in mushroom oil.

There are many more kinds of mushrooms, but varieties like chanterelle, morel, matsutake, black trumpet and porcini are pricey and/or labor intensive. I love them, but would rather have a half-pound of hydroponic maitake than an ounce of foraged morels. Depending on what kind of mushroom dish you're making, it may make more sense to use butter or animal fat instead of oil.

---

4 a.k.a., a Denver omelet.

SESAME-AVOCADO BROWN RICE

MAKES 4 SERVINGS | APPROXIMATE COST: $5-15 (DEPENDING ON GARNISHES)

I'd never heard of this specific combination before we served it at MSF, though intuitively, it seemed like an instant classic. It's low-prep, it's vegan, and it's served at room temperature. You can prep all of the components a day before serving, but don't dress the rice or cut the avocados until you're ready to go. We served it with a range of garnishes, but my personal favorite was broccoli rabe and broiled eel. Substitute toppings freely.

YOU WILL NEED:
- 2 CUPS BROWN RICE
- 2 LARGE, RIPE AVOCADOS
- ¼ CUP SOY SAUCE
- ¼ CUP RICE VINEGAR
- 3 TABLESPOONS SESAME OIL
- 2 TABLESPOONS SESAME SEEDS
- A 3.5-OZ PACKAGE OF BEECH MUSHROOMS
- I PACKAGE OF FROZEN JAPANESE BBQ EEL (OPTIONAL)
- I BUNCH BROCCOLI RABE (OPTIONAL)

I. Cook the rice in a pot or rice cooker.

2. Mix the liquid ingredients and season with a little salt. Toast sesame seeds and cool.

You can easily eyeball the proper water-to-rice ratio in a rice cooker by laying your hand flat on top of the rice. The resulting water level should be about an inch above the rice. For this dish, use slightly less water than usual, since you'll be moistening the finished product with the dressing. An hour before serving, remove rice from the rice cooker/warmer and cover it, allowing it to cool completely.

3. Trim the bottoms of the beech-mushroom clusters and separate the mushrooms.

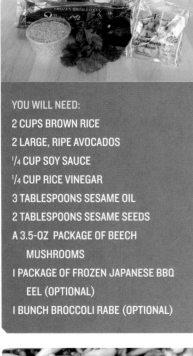

4. Sauté the mushrooms in a generous amount of oil; salt to taste.

5. Cut broccoli into bite-sized pieces. Blanch in heavily salted water (see page 159).

6. Shock broccoli in ice water. Gently wring to dry, then dress with olive oil and salt.

7. Thaw the eel and wipe off excess sauce. Slice in half lengthwise, then on a bias.

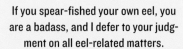

If you spear-fished your own eel, you are a badass, and I defer to your judgment on all eel-related matters.

8. Brown the eel under a broiler, or with a torch.

9. Shake the dressing vigorously and mix about half into the rice. Add more to taste.

10. The rice should be well coated, but not sopping wet. Fold in the sesame seeds.

11. Spoon out the avocados and cut into $1/2''$ chunks. Season them with salt.

12. Fold the diced avocados into the rice and transfer into serving bowls. Top with eel, broccoli rabe, beech mushrooms, and more sesame seeds.

TRIPLE-FRIED POTATOES

MAKES 6 SERVINGS AS A SIDE DISH, OR 30 SANDWICH TOPPINGS | **APPROXIMATE COST: $4 ($10, WITH FRYER OIL)**

I'll admit that these are actually just triple-cooked—not triple-fried. But "boiled and then double-fried potatoes" didn't have the same *je ne sais quoi*. Boiling softens and flavors the interiors; par-frying saturates the potatoes with oil; the final frying crisps the exteriors. This is an adaptation of Heston Blumenthal's method for "chips," which forgo the classic stick shape in favor of a sturdier and less wasteful wedge. I use Yukon Gold potatoes, which hold up to par-cooking relatively well and maintain structural integrity over time. Other varieties start to disintegrate as they cook.

YOU WILL NEED:

4 POUNDS PEELED POTATOES
(IF YOU'RE MAKING THIS AS PART OF
A FLATBREAD SANDWICH, ONE LARGE
POTATO WILL YIELD ENOUGH FOR
FIVE SANDWICHES)
I GALLON OF FRYER OIL

I. Quarter potatoes, then cut 1/3"-thick slices. Store in water to remove excess starch.

3. Simmer until the potatoes are soft enough to smush, but still hold their shape. Drain.

2. Place in a large pot of very salty water (as salty as you can stand to sip).

The potatoes are fragile, so drain carefully and cool them in a single layer. I like to pour par-boiled potatoes onto a big grate, so the water can drain and the potatoes have a lot of space to spread out, but you can use a slotted spoon or work in batches with a colander. Dumping a lot of potatoes into a small colander can result in a potato avalanche with a high casualty rate.

4. Par-fry at 275°F for 8–10 minutes. The exterior of the potato will form a "skin."

You can refrigerate the par-fried potatoes for a couple days or freeze them indefinitely. Now you may be thinking, "That's all well and good, but I don't have a fancy restaurant fryer—how am I supposed to monitor oil temperature?" Well, a countertop deep fryer only costs $40 and can easily control oil temperature. At MSF, we loved our little electric fryer and still use the same one we started with in the truck.

5. To serve, fry the potatoes again, this time at 350°F for 4 minutes, or until crispy.

CHARRED-SCALLION SOUR CREAM

MAKES 3 CUPS | APPROXIMATE COST: $8

Our neighborhood is full of taquerías where you can order *cebollitas*—charred scallions—as an accompaniment to your tacos. We use them often to add a pungent and smoky element to dishes. Jason Fox instructed his cooks to grill scallions until they're "as black as your soul" before blending them into a vinaigrette. We mixed them with sour cream and aioli to top our King Trumpet sandwich, served on a homemade flatbread (*see page 169*) with mushrooms, triple-fried potatoes (*see opposite page*), and garlic confit (*see next page*).

YOU WILL NEED:

3 BUNCHES SCALLIONS

½ CUP AIOLI OR MAYONNAISE
   (SEE PAGE 182)

2 CUPS SOUR CREAM

CHARCOAL

SMOKED SALT

BLACK PEPPER

I. Light a charcoal grill. At MSF, we improvised a grill using a wok or hotel pan and a grate from a home BBQ grill. This works great, if you've got proper ventilation.

2. Clean the scallions and cut off the bottoms.

3. Coat the scallions generously with olive oil and salt, and place them on a hot grill.

4. Grill the scallions until they're pretty black, but not actually catching on fire.

5. Mince the charred scallions.

6. Mix with the aioli and sour cream. Add smoked salt and black pepper to taste.

7. We served our charred-scallion sour cream with one of our sandwiches, but you could eat it with chips, gravlax, or on a hot dog.

━━━━━ **ACCOMPANIMENT** ━━━━━

GARLIC CONFIT

MAKES 1 POUND | APPROXIMATE COST: $5

Like Lionel Richie, garlic confit is soft, mellow, and easy like Sunday morning. If you make a large batch to keep on hand, you'll happen into plenty of uses for it.

YOU WILL NEED:

1 POUND WHOLE PEELED GARLIC CLOVES

OLIVE OIL

Garlic confit will keep indefinitely if the garlic is fully submerged in oil. Garlic oil is great for confiting cherry tomatoes, or sautéing vegetables.

1. Salt and place garlic cloves in enough oil to mostly cover. Simmer over low heat.

2. Once the cloves are soft and squishy, cool them and transfer to the fridge.

TAQUERÍA CANCÚN

Sure, you could eat at what was once Mission Street Food, or you could walk a few doors down and spend $7 per person at Cancún for one of the most satisfying meals available to a San Francisco diner.

(Above) Cebollitas *(grill-charred scallions).*

(Right) The elusive torta mojado *(available when the cooks feel particularly obliging).*

MSF RICE SAUCE

MAKES 3 CUPS | APPROXIMATE COST: $5

This is the recipe for the sauce we used in our signature duck-fat-fried rice. I initially tried to flavor the rice with a cold smoker—which looked like a marijuana pipe attached to a tiny motorized fan—but that was extremely time-consuming, and the rice didn't absorb much smokiness. Then I found that charred scallions and smoked salt imparted a full smoky flavor without the hassle. If you want to make a vegan version of this sauce, use soy sauce instead of fish sauce and add some rehydrated *konbu* for umami.

YOU WILL NEED:

3–4 BUNCHES OF CHARRED SCALLIONS
   (SEE STEPS 1–4, PAGE 165)
1 CUP MIRIN
1 CUP FISH SAUCE
SMOKED SALT
YOUR CHOICE OF ACCOMPANIMENTS
   FOR THE FRIED RICE

Add this sauce to flavor your fried rice toward the end of the cooking— mirin has a surprising amount of sugar, so it will burn before your rice has any crispiness. There's a point at which the flavor goes from smoky to carcinogenic, and duck fat can only do so much to mask it.

1. Purée whole scallions and liquids in a blender.

2. Blend until smooth, and season with smoked salt.

3. Garnish your fried rice with whatever combination of vegetables and meat you want. We topped ours with duck confit, crispy duck skins, seared cauliflower, and pickled celery.

BUTTERY FLATBREAD

MAKES 24 FLATBREADS | ESTIMATED COST: $5

For a long time, this was our proverbial and literal bread and butter. Methodologically, it resembles a scallion pancake, or *cong you bing*, but philosophically it follows the French principle of maximizing butter content. At MSF, the undisputed Commander of Flatbread was our sous-chef Emma Sullivan. We used to make as many as two hundred of these in a batch. After you make twenty-four, you'll understand why MSF opted for an early retirement.

YOU WILL NEED:

2 CUPS SIFTED AP FLOUR

2 CUPS SIFTED PASTRY FLOUR

I CUP CORNMEAL

I CUP BUTTERMILK

I CUP BOILING WATER

EXTRA FLOUR FOR DUSTING AND
   ADJUSTING

4–6 OZ TEMPERED BUTTER

24 6" x 6" SQUARES OF PARCHMENT
   PAPER, OR DELI PAPERS

SALT AND PEPPER TO TASTE

I. Mix the flours and cornmeal together in a large mixing bowl. Form a well in the center.

3. When the mix comes together, start kneading. Add more flour if it's too sticky.

2. Pour wet ingredients into the well and fold in the dry using a big spoon.

The goal is to knead the dough just enough so that it comes together, not so much that it gets tough. The perfect dough is as moist as possible without sticking—not unlike Play-Doh. Since your hands will be covered in sticky dough, test it on your arm or the back of your hand. Once you get it pretty close to ideal, it's okay to add a little more flour, since it gets stickier as it rests. But again, don't overwork it.

4. The key is to assess and adjust early in the kneading process.

5. The dough should come together just enough to form a ball.

6. Cover with plastic and rest at room temp for at least an hour, or up to 8 hours.

7. Portion the dough into 20–24 2-oz balls. Coat the balls by shaking in a cup of flour.

8. On a floured surface, roll the balls into thin disks. Work in batches of six.

9. Each disk should be about 6″ in diameter. Once rolled, peel the disks off the work surface so they don't stick, then lay them back down.

10. Spread tempered butter on one side of each disk. Sprinkle with salt and pepper.

11. Using your hands, roll each disk into a tube or cigar shape.

12. Roll or gently stretch the tubes into thinner tubes of about 12″–18″ in length.

13. Coil tubes into spirals like a cinnamon roll, and tuck the loose end underneath.

14. Flatten the spiral gently with your hand.

15. Flour generously.

16. Using the rolling pin, gently re-roll each coil into a 6″ disk.

17. Place each disk on parchment paper. Pile in bundles of up to 15 flatbreads.

18. Sear in a pan or on a griddle in oil, butter, or animal fat until browned on both sides.

19. Serve with escargots, Peking duck, or as a **PB&J** (see page 133–136) or the King Trumpet (see page 164–166).

EQUIPMENT LIST

In addition to standard equipment like knives, cutting boards, pots, and pans, there are some kitchen tools that are indispensable for cooking at a high level. With little more than these few items, you can turn your local Chinese dump into a charitable restaurant empire.

(A) **Whipped cream charger**: Not as ridiculous as you think. (*See page 180.*)

(B) **Torch**: A mini flamethrower. There are obvious uses, like crème brûlée, but it also comes in handy when you want to peel a tomato—just give it a quick singe and the skin will rub right off. The torch lets you apply high heat selectively, so you can toast a marshmallow right on top of a dessert. Or relight your stove's pilot light.

(C) **Chinois**: I identify with the chinois on a cultural level. Hmong other things, it's a sieve with an extra-fine mesh. Its conical shape allows you to expedite drainage by plunging liquid through with a ladle. Using a chinois is the secret to creating a truly smooth purée, thus putting the "fine" in "fine dining."

(D) **Tabletop Deep Fryer**: A steal at around $40, and an easy way to make things irresistible.

(E) **Powerful Blender**: A blender with at least 2 horsepower is useful to create a lot of fine-dining components. (*See page 174.*)

(F) **Mandolin and Microplane**: These allow you to easily cut yourself into thin slices, or very fine flakes. They also work on food.

G *Hotel Pans:* Home cooks have a variety of round pots and shallow rectangular baking pans, but not very many deep rectangular pans. Restaurants use 12" x 20" rectangular stainless steel vessels called hotel pans. Smaller versions are referred to by their fractional relation to a full-sized hotel pan. (A 12" x 10" pan is called a half pan, etc.) I think it's very useful to have a couple different depths of half pans and third pans (they come in 2", 4", and 6" depths), since a lot of foods (like slabs of pork belly) lend themselves to rectangular cooking vessels. Also, hotel pans come with lids, which simplifies matters when you're organizing your fridge or the trunk of your car.

H *Salad spinner:* You would never make a perfectly balanced vinaigrette and then dump a bunch of water in it, right? A salad spinner is like a little time machine that ensures that this never happens. It also lets you wash lettuce (or whatever else needs washing). The centrifugal force of the salad spinner has other applications as well—we've even used it to spin the grease out of some fried foods.

I *Spatula:* Heat-resistant silicon spatulas come in a variety of shapes and sizes, and are a lifesaver (if your life depends on getting every last bit of something out of a bowl).

J *Cooling racks:* Stainless-steel grates come in many sizes, and are useful for cooling, draining, or drying/salting. They're inexpensive, and it's nice to have them on hand in sizes that fit your refrigerator and pans. I keep one under my pillow, just in case.

SAUCES

Blenders and Purées

Armed with a powerful blender, you can make a lot of the components that separate fine-dining restaurants from Schmapplebee's or SchmeeGIFriday's. A good blender basically gives you the option of making anything into a sauce, soup, or spread. Though they cost about $400, they're totally worth it; I put one on our wedding registry. (But then those goobers at Bar Tartine ruined it. The motor on theirs had burned out because someone overloaded it with pistachios and hubris. We left our blender with them in the earliest days of MSF as collateral for using their kitchen. And within a week, some punk blended the plunger. Karen is still pretty peeved about it. Who do you think is writing this parenthetical section?)

I don't want to sound like an infomercial here, but the "3" in Vita-Prep 3 means three horsepower—the same as a chainsaw. Compare that to your 0.5-hp "pony" blender. The upside of that kind of power is that you can produce a velvety purée from mere carrots and water, but the downside is that the friction generates so much heat that you might inadvertently make carrot soup. As such, blender mastery revolves around minimizing unnecessary blending/heating, as well as minimizing the amount of added liquid (since you can always dilute with more liquid later).

The goal of power blending is to achieve a whirlpool action in which the contents are "turning over," circulating everything past the blades. Chef Jason Fox refers to this phenomenon as The Vortex.[5] Using the plunger, you can agitate and manipulate the contents vigorously while blending, which expedites your journey to The Vortex. Start on Low and fairly quickly turn up all the way to High, or pulse back and forth from Low to High to get the contents to shift around and incorporate. If you start on a setting that's too high, your contents will splash and you'll have to wipe down the edges of the pitcher with a spatula, so be cool, but not too cool, because you're on the clock and there's no point blending on Medium-Low for eight seconds while you build up the courage to shift to Max. After all, it's called the Vita-Prep 3, not Prince Wuss-o-Matic the Third.

The most important consideration is loading the blender with the right amount of material. If you're blending something that will become viscous (like nuts), or something delicate (like herbs), you should be careful not to overload the canister, because it might take too long for the contents on top to reach the desired consistency. But on the other hand, you need enough stuff in the canister for the whirlpool to form. Something between a pint and a quart is ideal. Start with some liquid at the bottom, since liquid turns

---

5 Vortices are not only central to his cooking, but also fundamental to his Philosophy of Life. (*See page 85.*)

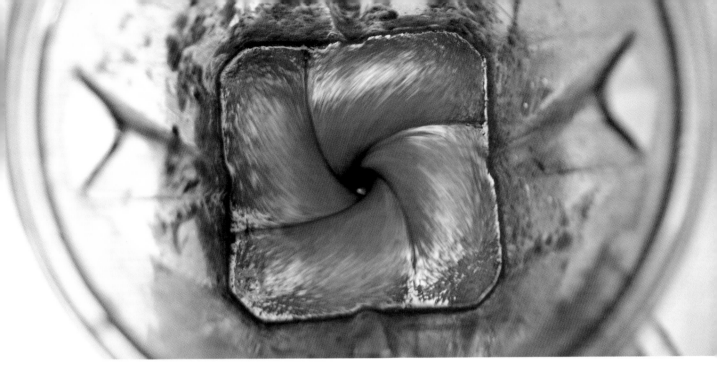

over immediately and any solid contents can settle into the resulting whirlpool. Think of it this way: if you're making pesto, and you load the oil last, it will just adhere to the basil leaves and nothing will turn over, and you'll end up adding more oil than you intended.

Other tricks of the trade that can be useful in particular circumstances:

- If you're making something fresh and delicate like cilantro water, you can add ice to the water to preempt cooking and maintain brightness.

- You can pre-cool the canister in the freezer to keep the temperature low—this is a good way to start a milkshake or a slushy cocktail.

- Heavy cream can become aerated in a powerful blender, so if you don't want to make flavored whipped cream, blend all of your other ingredients before incorporating the cream for the last few seconds.

Seafood purées are an underutilized type of sauce, in my opinion. We had fun experimenting with seafood purées at Mission Street Food. We puréed sea urchin and mixed it with softened butter to spread on crusty grilled bread; another time, we puréed barely cooked mussels to fold into lemony aioli to serve with skate. Here's one finding from that experiment: puréeing three pounds of mussels yields a pint of delicious sauce resembling loose diarrhea, yet if you snip the shit-sac off of each mussel prior to puréeing, the color improves but the sauce doesn't taste as good. Conclusion: mussel shit is the shit. Someday I'll try puréeing flying-fish roe with good olive oil to make a dressing—the possibilities are endless.

HOLLANDAISE AU BLENDEUR

MAKES 2 CUPS | **APPROXIMATE COST: $5**

The blender can be an efficient tool for making classic French sauces like Hollandaise and Béarnaise—a clever short-cut developed by Danny Bowien. In this recipe, the heat generated from the blender blades, coupled with warm butter, re-create the low-heat water-bath method traditionally used to emulsify butter sauces. Think of this as hollandaise, rejiggered for a bachelor-pad kitchen. (*Note: We conducted testing of this recipe in an actual bachelor pad.*)

YOU WILL NEED:

4 EGG YOLKS

1/2 TEASPOON DIJON MUSTARD

5 SHAKES OF TABASCO

2 TABLESPOONS LEMON JUICE

1 TABLESPOON WHITE WINE

2 CUPS MELTED BUTTER

UP TO 1 CUP WATER

1. Place all of the ingredients except butter and water in the blender and start on Low.

2. Microwave butter for 2 minutes. Make sure the butter's pretty hot, but not boiling.

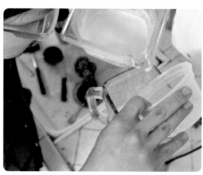

3. Gradually increase blender speed to High, and slowly introduce butter to emulsify.

4. Thin the sauce with water to achieve the desired consistency.

Traditionally, hollandaise is a little thinner than pancake batter, but you can experiment and decide what you prefer.

(For more on emulsions, see page 180.)

5. Let the entire mixture spin on High for 45 seconds to warm/cook.

If you're not serving the sauce immediately, transfer it into a container with a lid, or a thermos, and keep it in a hot-water bath until you're ready to serve. Take a moment to think of something witty to say in a French accent.

(ABOVE) CHEESE PIZZA, ARUGULA.   (BOTTOM) PETRALE SOLE, PURPLE POTATO, BRUSSELS SPROUT, JAMÓN CRISP, MARJORAM.

OYSTER TARRAGON PURÉE

MAKES I CUP | APPROXIMATE COST: $6

This is my version of a sauce they serve at Noma, the #1 restaurant in the world. We add oysters for depth and brininess, and to take the edge off of the tarragon. It's a complex sauce that could be used with elemental dishes like steak, fish, chicken, or omelettes. I apologize to René Redzepi and his staff, as I'm sure our version doesn't do justice to Noma's. Serve with musk-ox tartare, wood sorrel, and juniper if you want to bite Noma's style, or go off on your own if you think you're better than René Redzepi. At MSF, we couldn't get musk ox, so we used regular ox and Axe Bodyspray.

YOU WILL NEED:
BETWEEN ½ AND I BUNCH
    PICKED TARRAGON
4 OZ SHUCKED OYSTERS AND THEIR
    LIQUOR (½ A SMALL JAR OF
    OYSTERS)
12 OZ WATER
20 GRAMS AGAR (SEE PAGE 194)
SALT AND OLIVE OIL TO TASTE

I. Whisk the agar powder into I cup of cold water.

2. Whisk the mixture over high heat, allowing it to boil vigorously for 30 seconds.

3. Pour the agar mixture onto a plate and refrigerate to cool.

4. After an hour, the agar should be firm.

5. Use a quarter of the agar for this recipe. (See page 194 for other agar uses.)

6. Blend the agar, oysters, tarragon, a splash of olive oil, and a pinch of salt.

7. Store in the fridge. Now you know as much about Nordic cuisine as we do.

(ABOVE) NOMA'S MUSK-OX TARTARE.   (BELOW) ROAST BEEF SANDWICH.

Emulsions

Emulsions are molecular suspensions that can take one of two forms: fat surrounded by water or water surrounded by fat. A vinaigrette is a fat-in-water emulsion resulting in a translucent appearance and a silky mouth-feel; mayonnaise is a water-in-fat emulsion, resulting in an opaque appearance and a creamy mouth-feel. Fat-in-water emulsions are made by simple agitation, if the molecules fall out of suspension they can be re-emulsified by simply agitating again. Water-in-fat emulsions are more challenging because they require an additional emulsifier, like egg yolk, and if you're not careful, your ingredients can fall out of suspension, leaving you with just some eggy, watery oil.

Whipped Cream Chargers

I'm not saying you should go buy one, though they cost as little as $35. I mention them here to try and demystify the whole foam craze sweeping the fancy parts of the nation. Restaurants use chargers to aerate ingredients, which can create a pleasantly light texture—not unlike a dollop of whipped cream on your pie instead of a few glugs of heavy cream. But the real reason that chargers are ubiquitous in haute-cuisine kitchens is that they are a simple way to impress diners. I've never heard of a home cook busting out the charger for dinner, though it would be easy enough. Any liquid with a little protein and/or fat can serve as the basis for a foam, either on its own or with the addition of a stabilizer like gelatin. Just load the canister up, charge it with a couple nitrous cartridges, and you're ready to get all molecular up in there, like Dennis Hopper in *Blue Velvet*.

WHIPPED CREAM CHARGERS

(Opposite page) If the baristas at Starbucks can figure out how to use one, so can you.

FRESH MAYONNAISE

MAKES 4 CUPS | APPROXIMATE COST: $2–$10 (DEPENDING ON TYPE OF OIL)

This recipe doesn't specify a type of oil, but your choice will determine the flavor of your mayonnaise. Grapeseed or olive oil will yield a fairly neutral product—good on its own or as the basis for other flavors. Finely grate some fresh garlic into the mayonnaise for aioli, or make it "culturally diverse" with garam masala. You can also use premium oil if you want to really go for it. My *favorite condiment of all time* (!) is fresh mayo made with almond oil. You can control costs by blending premium oils with workaday olive oil.

YOU WILL NEED:

COLD WATER

3 EGG YOLKS

2 TEASPOONS DIJON MUSTARD

HEALTHY PINCH OF SALT

1/2 LEMON OR 1 TABLESPOON OF LEMON
    JUICE

3 CUPS OIL OF YOUR CHOICE
    (ALMOND OIL, ANYONE?)

1–2 CLOVES GARLIC (IF MAKING AIOLI)

3. As you add oil, the mixture should go from "sauce-like" to "pudding-like."

1. Combine yolks, salt, mustard, 1 tablespoon water, and lemon juice in a food processor.

2. Thoroughly mix to create a base, then, with the processor on, drizzle the oil in slowly.

4. The trick is to add oil gradually, and to keep the texture close to mayonnaise.

Making a mayonnaise emulsion starts by creating a mixture of emulsifier and water—the "base"—and then gradually adding oil while continuing to mix. I make fresh mayonnaise in a food processor. If you don't have one, or want to make a smaller batch, you can use a mixing bowl and a whisk. Secure your bowl by sitting it in a heavy pot lined with a damp dish towel.

Adding oil slowly (about 1 cup every 20 seconds) is especially critical in the early stages, because there's not much emulsified base and adding too much early on can overwhelm the proportions.

You may need to scrape down the sides at some point.

If the consistency seems thick, add a teaspoon or two of water, then another cup of oil, then a teaspoon or two of water, then the rest of the oil. That said, stiff mayo gives you some latitude to add condiments to your condiment.

(See Cilantro Aioli Variation, next page.)

But if an emulsion breaks completely, you'll be left with a bowl of dashed hopes.

Note: If all went well, the emulsion will appear opaque and cohesive. If you added too much oil, or poured too quickly, the mayonnaise can begin to "break." Don't worry, the party's not over yet. You can preserve a tenuous emulsion (shown above) by simply adding a splash of water.

Create a new base and introduce your old crestfallen mix as you would oil.

=== VARIATION ===

CILANTRO AIOLI

MAKES 4 CUPS | APPROXIMATE COST: $6

We put this on our signature sandwich, the PB&J (with pork belly, jicama, and pickled jalapeño), but it pairs well with a lot of things, from fried calamari to fried potatoes. A powerful blender outfitted with a plunger for agitating ingredients will make this recipe easier.

YOU WILL NEED:
2 BUNCHES CILANTRO
2 CLOVES OF GARLIC
I CUP OLIVE OIL
I TEASPOON LIME JUICE
TWO-FINGER PINCH OF SALT
2 CUPS MAYONNAISE OR AIOLI

I. Purée oil, garlic, and salt, then add cilantro (stems and all, if you have a good blender).

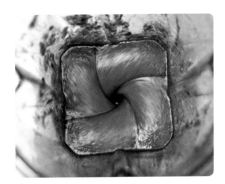

2. Alternate between the High and Low setting on your blender. Plunge vigorously.

3. Fold the resulting cilantro purée into fresh mayonnaise.

MOZZARELLA MOUSSE

MAKES 4 CUPS | APPROXIMATE COST: $6

Mozzarella mousse is pretty stable, like chocolate mousse, because it has a high fat and protein content. It's a decent way to approximate the luxury of burrata without the expense. Whereas good burrata can run upwards of $15 a pound at a specialty cheesemonger, the fresh mozzarella available at most supermarkets costs $3 to $6 a pound. Plus, you'll be significantly expanding the volume through aeration, so a little goes a long way (but it's still good even if you don't aerate it). Mozzarella mousse is nice with steak, charcuterie, fried potatoes, or as a creamy component in a salad.

YOU WILL NEED:

I LB FRESH WHOLE-MILK MOZZARELLA

I CUP HEAVY CREAM

CO_2 CHARGER

I–2 TABLESPOONS OLIVE OIL

SALT

1. Temper the mozzarella thoroughly, and chop into $1/4''$ chunks.

2. Pour cream and a splash of olive oil into the blender. Add the cheese on top.

It's important to temper and dice the mozzarella before blending it, so it's soft and blends easily. That way, you can use as little cream as possible, and avoid unnecessary dilution (or overblending for that matter).

Replace 2 ounces of the cream with buttermilk if you want to add some tang to the mousse.

3. Alternate between Low and High. Coax the mixture into turning over using the plunger.

4. Load mixture into the charger canister. Shake vigorously before each discharge.

5. Fresh mozzarella mousse will hold on the plate for at least 10 minutes.

(ABOVE) RADICCHIO, ALMONDS, MANDARINS, ESCAROLE. (BELOW LEFT) SERRANO HAM, OLIVES, MARCONA ALMONDS. (BOTTOM RIGHT) BOLOGNA, CRACKERS.

SEA FOAM

MAKES 8 SERVINGS OF DINNER-PARTY DRAMA | APPROXIMATE COST: $10 (PLUS GARNISHES)

This recipe is at the theatrical end of the foam spectrum. It's a great way to showcase the flavorful liquor that accompanies clams, but it would probably feel a bit ridiculous for a quiet dinner at home. Once discharged, the foam will dissipate dramatically into a satisfyingly clean, briny soup. Many chefs—José Andrés and David Chang come to mind—have employed this effect at their restaurants, but you can re-create it at home pretty easily. Hold a conch shell up to your guest's ear. Smile broadly and welcome them to Fantasy Island.

YOU WILL NEED:
2 POUNDS FRESH CLAMS, CLEANED AND
    PURGED THOROUGHLY
    (SEE PAGE 153)
1 CUP DASHI (SEE PAGE 192) OR WATER
3.5 SHEETS OF GELATIN OR 6.5 GRAMS
    GELATIN POWDER
CO_2 CHARGER
GARNISH OF YOUR CHOICE

Note: Clams can go from plump and juicy (clam on the left) to rubbery (clam on the right) very quickly. Ideally, stop cooking before the shells even open.

1. Blanch the clams in boiling water for 15 seconds to facilitate shucking.

2. "Unlock" the clams by inserting a butter knife and slicing the connective muscles.

3. Shuck the clams over an ice bath to catch and reserve their liquor.

2 pounds of clams should yield about a half cup of liquor.

Store the cooked, shucked clams and liquor in an ice bath to halt the cooking process.

4. Strain the clam liquor, and supplement it with dashi or water to make 1 pint of soup.

If the soup has any silt, you can remove it by straining through a coffee filter or by freezing the entire mixture in a flexible container; that way, you can pop the clamsicle out and chop off the silty layer at the bottom.

5. "Bloom" the gelatin sheets in cold water for a few minutes to soften them. Drain.

6. Warm your clam soup on the stove and add the gelatin sheets or powder.

7. Cool the soup until it sets.

8. Load the canister of the CO_2 charger with the gelatinized soup.

9. Charge it twice, shaking vigorously after each charge and before each discharge.

10. Place the chilled clams in a bowl. Garnish with edamame, crispy seaweed, sautéed ramps, cooked bacon, or anything resembling a coral reef. Top with sea foam.

BACON VINAIGRETTE

MAKES 12 SERVINGS | APPROXIMATE COST: $4

I only include a recipe for vinaigrette as a way of addressing the importance of balancing flavors—in this case, salty, acidic, and umami—and the many benefits of saving rendered fat. This is a variation on recipes I picked up from a couple of chefs I worked for, Collins Anderson and Jason Fox—both experts at slipping the pork into a saucy dish. For example, Jason dressed fresh shelling beans with bacon vinaigrette as an accompaniment to pork belly. But this vinaigrette is suitable for almost any salad.

YOU WILL NEED:

¼ CUP BACON GREASE

¼ CUP NEUTRAL-TASTING OIL

¼ CUP EXTRA VIRGIN OLIVE OIL

¼ CUP SHERRY VINEGAR OR APPLE
   CIDER VINEGAR

I TABLESPOON DIJON MUSTARD

SALT AND PEPPER TO TASTE

1. Whisk or blend all the ingredients together to form an emulsion. (See page 180.)

2. Dress whatever salad greens you have on hand. Bacon vinaigrette goes nicely with mixed chicories, sliced pear, goat cheese, and pumpkin seeds.

PANTRY

It takes savvy shopping and prep to ensure that a dish can be created "on the fly" and with minimal access to cooking equipment (as we had to do regularly at MSF). I liked to have the following items on hand as a kind of contingency plan.

From the store

Coconut milk: Cheap and vegan, cans of coconut milk are useful as the foundation of a dish, and they can be made even more decadent by reducing. Coconut milk brought down to one-third its original volume tastes as rich as Alfredo sauce. (Note: in my family, it's pronounced like Coco Chanel or Cocoa Puffs. As in, "The doctor told me to eat less Co-Co-nut. You take the leftovers home. I have to get ridth of it or I'll get diabetes.")

Fancy Oils and Vinegars: Everyone knows how to elevate a dish with a nice extra virgin olive oil, truffle oil, or aged balsamic vinegar, but not that many people branch out to things like hazelnut oil or aged rice vinegar. Priced at $10 to $20 per 500 ml, they're usually worth it, and the only danger is ending up with a jillion bottles on your shelf—the upper-middle-class foodie equivalent of cabinets full of canned goods. When the levees break, you'll still be living the good life.

Lemons/Limes: Sometimes you just really, really need one.

Miso: a rare combination of umami, veganism, and imperishability, miso can save you any time you need to add depth. Miso, butter, and a splash of sake immediately turns fish, chicken, or root vegetables into your very own Asian-Fusion Signature Dish.

Avocado: When you want to add richness or fat to a vegan dish (or any dish), it's nice to have avocados on hand. Make guacamole in less than a minute by halving, pitting, and smushing the halves against/through a small grate—creating a nice balance of smooth and chunky. Don't forget the salt. If you live outside the avocado belt, sorry for rubbing your face in it, but the rest of us have to live our lives, nahmean?

Herbs: Add complexity or freshness to almost any dish. Using fresh herbs is pretty much the only trick up my dessert sleeve (though my other sleeve contains triple-crème cheese). In addition to standbys like mint and basil, I like marjoram, tarragon, and oregano with various fruits. Asian herbs like shiso, rau ram, and ngo om (rice paddy herb) are really distinctive and aromatic. Apologies to Mentos, but cilantro is the real freshmaker, and I unapologetically add it to almost everything. Some people have a biological aversion to cilantro, so be mindful... of the company you keep.

Chicharrones: Added to a salad, they're like gourmet Bacos™, and they can also be used to add crunch factor. There are a wide range of textures from Funyuns™ to Werther's Originals™. I like the brand Anihaw, which are a good combination of crunchy and airy. Their salt-and-vinegar flavor has a nice sharpness that can be addictive.

Goat cheese: These days, goat cheese is fairly common, but it's still pseudo-sophisticated, melts easily, and it can be thinned with sour cream, milk, or cream into a sauce or spread as needed. An inexpensive and reliable brand is Laura Chenel's, which is available at Costco for $3.50 per 11-oz. log, and one goes a long way. Soon Costco will have a whole goat department, next to the cigarette cage, between optometry and the tire center.

Mascarpone and crème fraîche: These are useful thickeners, and can add depth or complexity to both savory and sweet dishes. You can make your own crème fraîche if you're so inclined. We did, and it simply involves leaving one part buttermilk and eight parts heavy cream in a non-metal container at room temperature or in a slightly warm place (like on top of a refrigerator) overnight, covered with a cheese-cloth or a napkin. Subsequent batches can be made with a one-to-one substitution of homemade crème fraîche for the butter-milk. This is not really a cost saver, but it makes you feel good about yourself. ("I'm a goddamn culinary MacGyver!")

Smoked Salt and Fish Sauce: Easy ways to add depth or an extra dimension.

Stabilizers: Agar, gelatin, and lecithin are useful to have on hand for emergency thickening, emulsifying, and stabilizing.

Eel and Co.: Serving a semi-exotic protein makes you seem like a good cook, and certain ones like eel allow you to put a delicacy on the table in just two minutes of active time. Eel is nice because it comes frozen, and thus has a good shelf life: thaw, wipe off the sweet sauce, slice, and broil. Just as easy and versatile, Spanish chorizo can be shaved and served cold, or it can be cut and crisped. Both proteins are assertive enough to elevate a dish, even as a secondary element. Some other fancy things with a good shelf life: squid ink, macadamia nuts, scented shelf-liners.

Basic Mise en Place

Mise en place is a French term which literally means "put in place." In practice, the terms refer to all of the components of your dish, from chopped onions to par-cooked bacon, once they've been fully prepped and are ready for their application in the final moment of cooking or plating. In restaurant kitchens, cooks spend the hours leading up to service preparing and assembling all of their "mise" so that it's on hand when they need it; you can do something similar at home by stocking up on some basic prepared ingredients that are versatile and durable. Sometimes prepping mise is as simple as saving your leftovers. (However, if, like me, you save weeks of pan drippings and then try to bring quarts of duck fat and gravy on a plane the day before Thanksgiving, you may find yourself at the mercy of your TSA agent's holiday spirit.)

The following prepared items would be reasonable for home cooks to keep in the refrigerator or freezer. Instead of starting from scratch for each meal, you can use these to improve the quality and increase the scope of a simple dish. You can also save time, money, and dish soap by cooking your components in larger batches.

Animal fat: Fat retains aroma better than water-based liquids. Whenever I'm making stocks or braising meats, I always try to save the fat. I prefer to amplify the specific flavor of a given meat by cooking it in its own fat. When cooked in animal fat, other foods, like onions, rice, or vegetables get more umami than their unanointed counterparts. For me, cooking with animal fats is an expression of my deep and abiding faith in science—that stem cells can clear my arteries faster than I can clog them.

Stock: A well-stocked kitchen should, as the term implies, be equipped with plenty of stock. Get in the habit of making stock, even from your scraps, just to have on hand—it doesn't have to be a big production. Other cookbooks will tell you how to make "perfect" stock, but I want to advocate making easy stocks all the time, rather than pristine stocks for special meals. Stock can be as simple as boiling your rotisserie chicken bones in a pot for a minute, turning off the heat, and covering.

Your stock will benefit from using meaty bones that are high in gelatin, as well as from the addition of vegetables or aromatics like onion, leek, carrot, fennel, bay, garlic, etc. Even if you're making a nice stock, you don't necessarily need to spend hours skimming and fussing over it. You can use a pressure cooker, or just throw a whole roasting pan with your components in the oven for a few hours at 300°F; strain through a chinois to remove solids.

If you want to really go for it, there are a few additional options. You can roast your bones prior to making stock, which significantly deepens the flavor. You can wash your meat and bones beforehand,[6] but I'm usually content to remove the impurities settled at the bottom and just under the fat layer of fully cooled stock. You can even go all the way and clarify with an egg-white raft (Google "consommé recipe" and just be careful not to scorch the egg whites).

For mushroom stock, boil water with mushroom stems for 20 minutes. Mushroom stock is a great basis for fortification—just use it instead of water when making stock or soup. Likewise, make any stock a dashi by bringing to a boil, removing from the heat, and adding a piece of konbu (and a big handful of bonito flakes, if you like).

---

6 Or even bring them to a boil for a couple minutes, then discard that water.

Cover and let steep for an hour or two, straining when the dashi is sufficiently flavorful.

Pickles: Can provide the all-important contrast necessary to refresh your palate and make you want more of the rich stuff. In recent years, Eurocentric haute cuisine has really embraced pickling (which has always been a central part of Eastern cuisine).

Watery vegetables like cucumbers are best when simply salt-pickled, with acid added only right before serving. Salted vegetables get funkier and more ferment-y the longer you leave them at room temperature. You can experiment with varying degrees of the kimchi/sauerkraut effect to find a level of pungency that suits you and your milieu.

Root vegetables, like beets, carrots, and ginger seem to hold indefinitely when pickled in a traditional vinegary brine. I recommend cutting back or even omitting the sugar from most pickle recipes. You can always add a pinch of sugar later, but honestly, I've never thought, "The problem with these pickles is that they're not sweet enough." Karen is not naturally fond of vinegary pickles, but she's made some progress since we've been together. And that's what love is all about, folks.

Bacon: Sliced and frozen or cooked and cooled, bacon keeps pretty much indefinitely and is always a crowd-pleaser. You can throw it in a pasta dish or some cookie dough on a whim. The smokiest bacon I've ever had comes from Benton's Smoky Mountain Country Hams in Nashville, Tennessee. You can use their website, but the gentleman who answers the phone (403-540-3853) illustrates what people mean by Southern hospitality. Benton's is a great ingredient-bacon because it's extremely salty and smoky, but it might be overwhelming in a monster BLT.

Mushrooms: I have never encountered a dish with too many mushrooms. Not ever. I like to prepare and cook more mushrooms than I need because I invariably find a way to use them later. Sometimes, I bring them to the pizza place. Seriously. I always save the stems for making a quick broth that keeps indefinitely and can be used in place of water any time I want more umami. See the mushroom guide in the vegetable section (*page 161*). This entry is just to remind you to buy extra mushrooms.

Seaweed: Toasted nori and certain dried seaweed varieties are delicious on their own, with rice, or in a sandwich, but they can also be pulsed into a powder and used as a topping. It's very worthwhile to fortify broths with a little sea lettuce or konbu, right along with your carrots and onions.

Garlic confit: While not a substitute for fresh garlic and its distinctive punch, garlic confit can add last-minute depth to a soup or complexity to a sandwich. Simmer whole cloves slowly in oil, transfer to the fridge with enough oil to fully submerge, and keep indefinitely. Any extra garlic oil is also good for cooking vegetables and eggs. (*See page 166.*)

Advanced Mise en Place

Gelatin purée: Most kitchens discard things like chicken skin or pork skin after they've made stock. I recommend reserving these, blending them with a little bit of stock, straining, and freezing the resulting purée. This suggestion is a prime example of the intersection between scrappiness and refinement that MSF was all about. Sure, you're not going to cloud your consommé or demi-glace with puréed chicken skin. But you can improve your meatloaf, gravy, or soup 10 percent. And sometimes you just need a quick fix. If your braised pork shoulder is dry, add a cup of gelatin to the re-warming liquid to introduce unctuousness; if you have a thin braising liquid that's too salty to reduce into a viscous sauce, voilà, gelatin purée to the rescue.

Agar brick: I admit, this is beyond advanced home cooking, but there are a lot of situations in which you want to thicken a sauce. In molecular gastronomy, a sauce thickened with agar is called a fluid gel. Once set, agar doesn't lose its structural integrity—it just becomes smaller and smaller bits of gel, which means you can blend agar with thin liquids like balsamic vinegar, soy sauce, or cilantro water to increase their viscosity.

The conventional approach is to add an exact ratio of agar powder to the liquid you're trying to thicken, heat it, let it cool and set, then blend it. That's a good approach if you have a perfect recipe for a soy sauce fluid gel (something not hurt by heat), but not great if you're making a cilantro fluid gel (something hurt by heat) or a balsamic fluid gel (since balsamic varies in viscocity depending on the vinegar quality). Unless you have a tested recipe, you may end up wasting a lot of time before you hit the right consistency.

A more forgiving approach is to make a concentrated agar brick, using 20 grams of agar powder per 12 oz of water, boiling it for 30 seconds, and then letting it cool into a really firm brick. This allows you to add agar piece by piece to achieve the desired consistency.[7] Using my approach, you can make it perfect it in 30 seconds, rather than starting over. You'll also be able to thicken something (below 180°F) on a whim that you hadn't been planning to turn into a fluid gel.

Charred Vegetables: Can be chopped or puréed into a sauce (*see pages 165–168*), or can be burnt to a crisp to make powder. If you have a grill going, you might as well char some scallions and reserve them. You can also harvest vegetable ash from scraps like carrot peels or onion skins: place the scraps in a sieve or colander over the grill, char them black, and shake the colander over a mixing bowl to collect the resulting bits of ash. Grind the ashy bits with some salt in a spice mill or blender. Use vegetable ash to coat anything you want to make black and smoky without actually charring, like a piece of gently steamed fish, goat cheese, or cucumber.

---

7 The trade-off is that while you'll get the right consistency, you'll be introducing slightly more water to your gel.

DESSERT

I admit it: my favorite dessert is a bowl of cereal with a few teaspoons of ice cream added to the milk. Specifically, I like Honey Bunches of Oats with Almonds and Breyers Natural Vanilla ice cream. (Don't knock it till you've tried it!) Granted, this is hardly the stuff of cookbooks, but cereal-with-ice-cream does reflect our broader philosophy of cooking: adding a complementary texture, an accent flavor, or a new technique is all it takes to elevate a dish.

In savory food, we all know that it makes sense to put a slice of cheese on a burger because we've been socialized. It's called a cheeseburger. Of course, there's something complementary about the flavors, too, but for some reason, unless you're at a Michelin-starred restaurant, dessert experimentation runs pretty close to the straight and narrow. For example, not very many people throw triple-crème cheese on their brownies—perhaps also because they've been socialized. It's called common decency.

But upon further consideration, this makes no sense. We put icing on cake, right? And what is fancy cheese if not the icing of the Gods? So I say go for it: "frost" a brownie with Camembert. And while you're at it, live a little. Freeze a foie gras torchon and shave curls of it onto ice cream. Top a snickerdoodle with jalapeño-sugar. Carbonate your lychees.

But apart from simply encouraging

A BALANCED BREAKFAST

With your recommended daily allowance of cooking philosophy in every bowl.

experimentation, I'm also a proponent of layers. If you like mango with sticky rice, float it in a pool of coconut water. If you like fresh strawberries, serve them with strawberry Pop Rocks. If you like chocolate ice cream, top it with sage and extra virgin olive oil.

This section presents a few simple but rewarding recipes. Most are nothing more than a single technique or flavor combination that we turned to often at Mission Street Food. We threw a lot of desserts against the wall, but these were the ones that stuck.

BROWN-BUTTER FINANCIER

MAKES 12 SERVINGS | APPROXIMATE COST: $8

This cake recipe is simple, versatile, and delectable. It has a pleasing ratio of chewy interior to crusty exterior, splitting the difference between a sponge cake and a cookie. For me, the chance to use up some egg whites is a nice bonus, but maybe that's just because I have dozens of egg whites in my fridge at any given time.

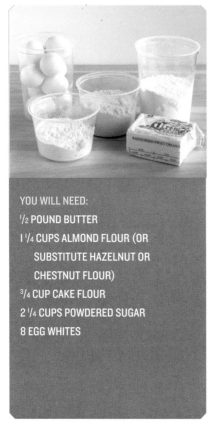

YOU WILL NEED:
1/2 POUND BUTTER
1 1/4 CUPS ALMOND FLOUR (OR SUBSTITUTE HAZELNUT OR CHESTNUT FLOUR)
3/4 CUP CAKE FLOUR
2 1/4 CUPS POWDERED SUGAR
8 EGG WHITES

1. Heat the butter in a saucepan until it turns brown and nutty, stirring frequently.

2. Place the almond flour on a parchment-lined tray and bake at 350°F until golden.

3. Grease a 9" x 12" pan with oil or butter, and line with parchment paper.

4. Sift the cake flour and combine with the toasted almond flour.

5. Mix in a stand mixer with the whisk attachment for 30 seconds.

6. Add the egg whites and mix for a few minutes, until thoroughly incorporated.

7. Add butter (including browned bits) and mix thoroughly. Then add powdered sugar.

Test for doneness by inserting a tooth-pick. If it comes out cleanly (without any moist cake batter), the cake's done. Unlike some prima-donna cake batters, this one will keep in the refrigerator for a couple of days. Once it's baked off, it'll stay pretty fresh if you wrap it tightly, too.

8. Once the sugar is incorporated, pour the batter into the lined baking pan.

9. Bake for about 30 minutes at 350°F.

10. This thin cake is extremely versatile as a base for almost any ice cream, and pairs well with a variety of fruits. The above combination—blueberries, mint ice cream, mint leaves, and pine-nut brittle—was completely random, but it tasted as good as it looks.

STRAWBERRY, SORREL, CRÈME FRAÎCHE

MAKES 4 SERVINGS | APPROXIMATE COST: $8

This is not so much a recipe as it is a flavor combination. To me, it's the dessert equivalent of tomato, basil, and mozzarella—a perfect combination that you can take credit for at every opportunity until it gets played out after a few years. The grassiness of the sorrel and the richness and tang of the crème fraîche make a nice backdrop for the sweetness of the strawberries. If your strawberries are not very delicious, you can improve their flavor by adding some sugar and macerating them in sauternes or something else really expensive.

YOU WILL NEED:

1 PINT STRAWBERRIES, TOPPED AND CUT INTO QUARTERS

2 PACKED CUPS SORREL

1 CUP WATER

1–2 TEASPOONS GRANULATED SUGAR

1/2 A SET AGAR BRICK (SEE PAGE 178)

1 CUP CRÈME FRAÎCHE

1–2 TABLESPOONS POWDERED SUGAR

1. Blend the sorrel leaves and stems with the water, sugar, and agar.

Add a splash of water and a bit of agar at a time. The consistency should be a little thinner than ketchup. If the mixture is chunky, pass it through a fine-mesh strainer.

2. Sift powdered sugar through a sieve, and whisk into the crème fraîche to taste.

3. Pair with griddled cornbread (see next page) to create a thinking man's strawberry shortcake. Blackberries make a nice substitute for the strawberries.

GRIDDLED CORNBREAD

MAKES 24 SMALL SLICES | APPROXIMATE COST: $7

This recipe comes from a former coworker, Brook Gossard, who was a paragon of grace under pressure (the pressure of kitchen life and of the human condition generally). After a considerable amount of analysis, I determined that it would be good to griddle it in butter. Ideally, top it with something creamy and something sweet, like honey. It's a good accompaniment to the buttermilk panna cotta (*see next page*), and would be a good vehicle for strawberries, crème fraîche, and sorrel (*see previous page*).

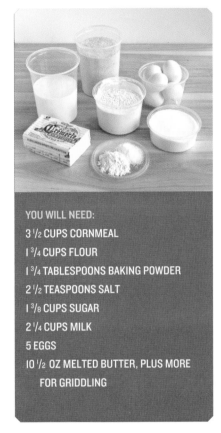

YOU WILL NEED:

3 ½ CUPS CORNMEAL

1 ¾ CUPS FLOUR

1 ¾ TABLESPOONS BAKING POWDER

2 ½ TEASPOONS SALT

1 ⅜ CUPS SUGAR

2 ¼ CUPS MILK

5 EGGS

10 ½ OZ MELTED BUTTER, PLUS MORE
    FOR GRIDDLING

1. Butter a 9" x 12" pan, and line it with a piece of parchment paper.

2. Whisk the sugar, milk, butter, and eggs together.

3. Mix the dry components in a separate mixing bowl and make a well in the center.

4. Pour the wet components into the well. Mix as little as needed to fully incorporate.

5. Fill the pan and bake at 425°F for 35 min. If it browns too quickly, cover with foil.

6. Rotate once. It's done when an inserted toothpick comes out completely clean.

7. Allow to cool before portioning. Fry slices in a nonstick pan with some butter.

BUTTERMILK PANNA COTTA

MAKES 12 SERVINGS | APPROXIMATE COST: $8

I adapted this recipe from a pastry-chef friend. (Thanks, ML!) We served it successfully with a variety of accompaniments, ranging from cornbread fried in butter (*see previous page*), to a mélange of fresh peas, pea leaves, celery hearts, celery leaves, chervil, and mint oil, in another homage to a dish they serve at Noma. (Thanks, Chef René!) This is the quintessential MSF dessert, because it's inexpensive, simple, versatile, and seems sophisticated—the tang of the buttermilk and the richness of the cream add up to a kind of Euro-fro-yo. It's not embarrassing, though, because you call it panna cotta.

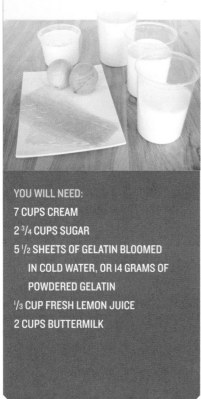

YOU WILL NEED:

7 CUPS CREAM

2 ³/₄ CUPS SUGAR

5 ¹/₂ SHEETS OF GELATIN BLOOMED
   IN COLD WATER, OR 14 GRAMS OF
   POWDERED GELATIN

¹/₃ CUP FRESH LEMON JUICE

2 CUPS BUTTERMILK

1. Combine the lemon juice and buttermilk in a big bowl or bucket.

2. Over medium heat, warm cream and sugar just below a simmer. Turn off the heat.

3. Whisk the gelatin (strained first, if you're using sheets) into the cream thoroughly.

4. Slowly pour the hot cream into the buttermilk-lemon mix and stir gently.

5. Portion the panna cotta mixture into vessels and refrigerate.

There are two basic ways to serve panna cotta: in their individual vessels or inverted onto a plate. If you choose the former presentation, pour the liquid into service vessels and leave them in the refrigerator until they've set. This can take as little as 3 hours, but it will depend on your fridge. Panna cotta can hold for several days, so you may as well refrigerate it, covered, overnight to be safe.

If you opt for a plated presentation, portion the liquid into disposable cups and refrigerate as described above. When you're ready to serve, run a knife along the inside perimeter of the cup before placing it upside down on a plate. Cut a slit in the base of the cup to let in air and un-suction the panna cotta. You may have to kind of squish or jostle the cup a little to release the contents.

(ABOVE) WITH SPRING VEGETABLES AND HERBS.   (BELOW) WITH HUCKLEBERRY COMPOTE AND TARRAGON-SUGAR-COATED CHEX.

BROWNIES

MAKES 12 HUGE BROWNIES | APPROXIMATE COST: $16 (PLUS ANOTHER $30 FOR CHEESE AND NUT TOPPINGS)

I settled on this recipe after exhaustive trial and error, not unlike an honest-to-goodness pastry chef. (My complete lack of baking knowledge lends credibility to my claim of exhaustiveness.) I'm biased, but I think this recipe has the perfect balance of brownie textures—cakey and fudgy, with that distinctive papery brownie business on top. Flavorwise, it offers a sophisticated conjunction of dark chocolate and vanilla with a little pizzazz from the crème fraîche. We served these with toasted hazelnuts and extremely generous slabs of Brillat-Savarin cheese (for even more 'zzazz).

YOU WILL NEED:

10 ½ OZ HIGH-QUALITY BITTERSWEET
    CHOCOLATE (IN THE 70% RANGE)
14 OZ BUTTER
3 ½ TEASPOONS VANILLA EXTRACT
7 EGGS
⅓ CUPS COCOA POWDER
2 ¾ CUPS SUGAR
EXTRA SUGAR AND COCOA FOR DUSTING
⅔ CUP CRÈME FRAÎCHE OR SOUR CREAM
1 ⅔ CUPS FLOUR
1 ¼ TEASPOONS SALT

1. Melt the chocolate and butter in a double boiler, or in a microwave on the low setting.

2. Whisk the eggs with the crème fraîche (or sour cream), sugar, and vanilla.

3. Add the butter and chocolate to the mix.

4. Sift and mix the cocoa, flour, and salt in a separate bowl. Form a well in the center.

5. Pour the wet ingredients into the well in the center of the dry ingredients.

6. Gradually incorporate all of the dry ingredients, mixing as little as possible.

Don't overmix the batter, but be sure to incorporate all of the dry ingredients into the wet ones, taking care to scrape the bottom of the bowl.

7. Butter a 9″ x 12″ baking pan and dust it with cocoa. Shake out the excess cocoa.

8. Fill the cocoa-dusted pan with the batter.

9. Sprinkle the entire surface evenly with several big pinches of granulated sugar.

10. Bake for 24–30 minutes at 350°F.

11. Check for doneness every few minutes thereafter.

Be careful not to overcook. Overcooked brownies are just dense cake. The goal is for the middle to be a bit fudgy, so if you insert a toothpick into the brownies, it should come out a little dirty, but not with any liquid batter on it.

Allow the brownies to cool before slicing them.

DARK-CHOCOLATE MAGIC SHELL

MAKES SIX CUPS | APPROXIMATE COST: $15

Magic shell has been shut out by the snotty maître'd's of haute cuisine, just because the name's a little childish. But dip $1 bills in it and you can sell them for $5. For a quick catering canapé, we dipped store-bought cream puffs in magic shell, and topped them with cocoa nibs before the shell hardened. We called them profiteroles; one woman said she ate twenty-three. The idea with this recipe is that the fat makes the chocolate thin and stable, so you can use it in a variety of applications.

YOU WILL NEED:

1 1/2 POUNDS DARK CHOCOLATE

1 POUND COCONUT OIL, LARD, OR
    ANY FAT THAT IS SOLID AT ROOM
    TEMPERATURE

COLD OR FROZEN ITEMS FOR DIPPING
    (LIKE STORE-BOUGHT CREAM PUFFS)

1. Melt the chocolate and fat in a double boiler, or in a microwave set on Low.

2. Whisk. Then dip frozen items using toothpicks.

3. Mount on styrofoam, and then freeze to allow the shell to harden.

4. Feel free to get creative. Squirt drips of magic shell into ice water to make chocolate squiggles, or brush it on toasted filo to make sheets of chocolate crisp (pictured above).

FRENCH TOAST CRUNCH

MAKES 4 SLICES | APPROXIMATE COST: $10

The French term for French Toast is *pain perdu*, which literally means "bread lost (in sugary scrambled eggs)." This variation caramelizes the bread and the sugar, skips the egg entirely, but remains loyal to its Gallic roots, with a liberal amount of butter and the use of brûlée, which is French for "bejazzle."

YOU WILL NEED:

A LOAF OF STURDY PAN DE MIE
    (OR 4 SLICES OF TEXAS TOAST)
½ CUP TEMPERED BUTTER
2 CUPS GRANULATED SUGAR
2 CUPS HALF AND HALF
3–4 OZ CONDENSED MILK

1. Slice bread into ¾" to 1" slabs.

2. Spread 2 tablespoons of butter on each slice of bread. (It's okay. This is dessert.)

3. Toast or bake the buttered bread until the edges are lightly browned.

4. Put the sugar in a shallow container or on a plate. Dip each piece of toast in sugar, then sprinkle on a bit more to coat evenly.

You can use your torch's maximum flame setting. Keep the nozzle about 2–3 inches from the toast. Tip your baking sheet to coax melted sugar toward unmelted sugar. Avoid torching the edges, because unsugared bread can ignite.

5. Place the toast on a metal rack set over a sheet pan. Melt sugar with a torch.

6. Keep the flame moving across the surface of the toast to avoid burning one spot.

7. Stop torching before the sugar turns dark brown. It will continue to darken on its own.

8. Whisk condensed milk into the half and half to reach desired sweetness.

9. Place each piece of brûléed toast in a hefty puddle of sweetened half and half.

A FEW POSSIBLE FRENCH TOAST CRUNCH VARIATIONS

TYPE	NAME	METHOD
Indian	Cardamom Toast Crunch	Sprinkle cardamom on toast*; add yogurt to half and half
Irish	Bailey's Toast Crunch	Add Bailey's to half and half; use potato bread
Mexican	Horchata Toast Crunch	Add horchata to half and half; sprinkle cinnamon and cocoa on toast*
Japanese	Matcha Toast Crunch	Add matcha to half and half; neatly cut off bread crust
French	French French Toast Crunch	Substitute cream for half and half; double the amount of butter
Pirate	Rum Raisin Toast Crunch	Use raisin bread; add grog to half and half
Breakfast	Cinnamon Toast Crunch	Sprinkle cinnamon on before sugaring toast*
Vegan Breakfast	"Cinnamon Toast Crunch"	Use focaccia and margarine for bread and butter; sprinkle cinnamon on toast*; use sweetened soy-milk instead of dairy
Thai	Kaffir Toast Crunch	Substitute coconut milk for half and half; infuse with kaffir lime leaves
Italian	Amaretto-Mascarpone Toast Crunch	Add amaretto to half and half; frost bread with mascarpone before sugaring
Greek	Baklava Toast Crunch	Flavor half and half with honey and rose water; garnish with pistachio
Christmas	Eggnog Toast Crunch	Use eggnog instead of half and half; sprinkle nutmeg on toast*
Tropical	Banana-Coconut-Cilantro Toast Crunch	Spread banana on toast; use coconut milk; garnish with cilantro

Always add spices before sugar. Spices will burn.

THE MSF MANUAL
(AN ODE TO THE KLF)

In 1988, the British band The KLF published a tongue-in-cheek (yet utterly serious) guide to dominating the pop charts. In The Manual (How to Have a Number One the Easy Way), *Bill Drummond and Jimmy Cauty offered a one-week guide from penury to celebrity. Drummond later summarized* The Manual's *advice: "If you want to do something, go and do it! Don't wait to be asked, don't wait for a record company to come and want to sign you or a management company. Just go and do it... If you wanna have number one... you can have it. It won't make you rich, it won't make you happy, but you can have it."*

The KLF are known for multiple appearances at number one on the UK billboard charts, as well as for publicly deleting all of their music, burning one million pounds sterling, and founding the K Foundation, which hosted an award ceremony for worst artist of the year in the Tate Modern.

This book is ostensibly supposed to present the aspiring restaurateur with ideas for re-creating MSF's success. But writing a serious list of steps to opening a restaurant seemed obnoxious, and the restaurant industry could afford to shed some self-seriousness. We like that the KLF's Manual *was part art project, part subversive social criticism, part irreverent joke, and part practical guidebook. Thus, we herewith present* The MSF Manual (An Ode to The KLF), *a half-serious, fully obnoxious list of steps to restaurant success.*

BE READY TO BASK IN THE GLORIES OF MOTHER NATURE'S BOUNTY

Be ready to satisfy the sensory desires of throngs of eager customers. Be ready to live the dream, because it is only by following the clear and simple instructions contained in this manual that you can realize your inexplicable desire to become a successful chef and secure your place in the annals of food history.

Other than chefhood, we offer you nothing else. There will be no boundless wealth. Fame will pass like nectarine season, and sexual relations will still be frustrating and unsubstantial. What you painstakingly created will be greedily swallowed and eventually bastardized by housewives and (more) exploitative food personalities.

But while we all know that a recipe is not going to save the world, it will temporarily occupy the mind and the mouth of some individual whose mind and mouth sought occupation. Ever after, such individuals will huddle together in the booths of gastro-pubs far and wide with sepia-toned memories of melting, crispy, creamy, savory delights. So rest assured that your efforts were not in vain, though—in fact, vanity is the driving force.

People equate being a successful chef with excitement, recognition, glory. Oddly, they even attribute an undeserved degree of sexiness to chefs. Like reality-TV personalities, poker players, and certain celebrity animals, successful chefs are seen as experiencing a desirable lifestyle. In fact, in the eyes of the food press, the more egregious a chef's pursuit of trivial perfection, substance abuse problems, or issues with hygiene or obesity, the more compelling that lifestyle becomes.

Successful chefdom is seen as the apex of the culinary arts.

The truth is that most successful chefs are merely in the business because their educational backgrounds were not strong enough to keep them out of the service industry. And if one of these aimless schlubs does stumble into success, he will eventually hire some underling to run his kitchen, thereby earning the disdain of his "more serious" colleagues, who relentlessly shit-talk any chef unsuspecting enough to wander outside of earshot. These "serious chefs" can be seen making the rounds at your city's highest-priced farmers' market.

Of course there are the rare, talented, committed individuals who give themselves over to being chefs. These masochistic souls experience success as Siamese twinhood—resignation to a life sentence, joined at the hip with their kitchens. Perfection is literally a flash in the pan of their intense focus before they move on to the next fetishistic quest.

So why bother? If becoming a successful chef is either pointless or a curse, what good can come of it?

Well, what the fuck else are you gonna do? Become a startender?

So how do you go about becoming a successful chef?

First, you must be unemployed in a long-term way. If you have a job or even job prospects, you will choose them over the toil of the kitchen. Ideally you've washed out of another career so you know that no better options await. Second, you must be broke, because if you have any kind of real savings, you'll probably prefer to coast on the assumption that something more promising will come your way. Being poor also instills a disdainful freedom from the concerns of your eventual clientele, providing the kind of clarity necessary to make decisions under the pressure of real constraints.

If you happen to be enrolled at culinary school, stop attending. Better yet, get ready to categorically write off everything you learned there. Your knowledge of food safety and your hours of training to work under a negligible amount of pressure constitute serious obstacles to your more realistic and caffeinated peers.

Your school will be the Internet. Remember, the Internet is the world's official record of existence, and taking the antiquated "Fuck bloggers/Yelp" stance only gets you the title of private chef. We repeat, stroke the Internet like your new lover and learn what makes it happy, because there's no denying the fact that you're in bed together.

YOU CAN START ANY TIME

Open your browser and, using a search engine like Google, type "best restaurant" and the name of your chosen city. Once you've identified that restaurant, or better yet, narrowed the field to, say, the five best restaurants, start by reading their menus and reviews. This should provide you with an understanding of what your customer base finds appealing and acceptable. In order to become a successful chef, you will simply have to provide something that is more desirable than what is being offered by these restaurants. In many cases, this is as easy as it sounds.

If you started in the morning or afternoon, you're probably ready for lunch or dinner. Go to the best fast-food place in your neighborhood—ideally a Popeyes or In-n-Out Burger. If you don't have one in your area, the neighborhood McDonald's will suffice. Order something simple but good, like a double cheeseburger, some McNuggets, and some fries. After you finish your meal, think about how satisfying it was, and how the experience compares to "fancier" food you've had in the past, and how it cost only about $3.

Now that you're not hungry any more, go to one of the "best restaurants" that you read about on the Internet. If you need to change into the proper attire, head home and get ready first. When you arrive, tell the host or hostess that you're waiting for someone. If they offer you a spot at the bar, accept it, or else after a moment ask to use the restroom. Once inside, take a look at the menu and the food that people are eating. Memorize it. If you can see the kitchen, get as close as possible and watch how the cooks are working. If you're so inclined, you could eat something, but it's optional. If there was more than one restaurant on your list, visit the others and repeat.

The next day, go back to the restaurant you found to be the most impressive for one reason or another. Tell them they're your favorite restaurant in the city, you love their [insert signature dish], and offer to work for free. Tell them how excited you are to work in their restaurant, and how you will gladly pick herbs or do anything else they want you to. If they ask you about your prior experience, say you used to work at some places in another city across the country. You can make up some generic respectable-sounding name, like "The Park City Grill" or "Regency Café." Pick a reputable city, but one where no one's familiar with the food, like Miami or Toronto.

Once you've successfully obtained an unpaid position at the restaurant of your choice, don't say anything that will blow your cover. If you actually know more than someone about something, don't flaunt it. Shut up, watch, and learn. Eventually you'll get an opportunity to cook something. This may take months or years, depending on what kind of restaurant you chose and how understaffed they are.

After an additional one to five years spent mastering everything the restaurant serves, you're ready to become a successful chef. Keep in mind how satisfying that fast food was.

Your goal is to make the most desirable food—and given virtually no resources, don't bother trying to do what the current best restaurants are doing. If the best restaurants in your city serve expensive ingredients, prepared simply, think about serving cheap ingredients prepared with consummate skill. If the best places boast white tablecloths and great wine pairings, think about serving food in an off-kilter environment alongside cheap beer. If the best restaurants have established chefs and serve tried-and-true recipes, think about changing the menu every night and involving unreliable and unproven chefs.

Those are just examples of how to approach the task of serving food more desirable than what the current best restaurants offer. Though the process is nuanced, and there are many wrong answers, there are also many right answers. For example, Korean tacos sound shamelessly gimmicky, but no one noticed, and the chef who popularized them has already become the object of envious shit-talking by countless other successful chefs. You could be next.

THE FOUR GOLDEN RULES OF THE SUCCESSFUL CHEF

Since you're broke and underqualified, you'll need to focus on only the bare minimum needed to achieve success. We'll start with a kitchen. While it would be nice to have a fully equipped professional kitchen at your disposal, you can make do with almost anything. Start a conversation with any restaurant owner, caterer, food-truck operator, warehouse owner, or even someone with a nice apartment. Tell them you're an accomplished chef and you're going to make a lot of money and will give them some of it to use their space.

While there are a lot of technicalities to consider before starting a food business, like operating permits and workers' compensation, you can figure that stuff out later. The important thing is to nail down a kitchen and then start applying the Golden Rules of the Successful Chef.

The Four Golden Rules are as follows:

1. UMAMI

Umami is the fifth flavor; it literally means "satisfying like meat." It was officially recognized only in the last twenty or so years by the West, but has been well known in Eastern cultures for hundreds of years. Aside from having a word for it, the Japanese also invented a synthetic version (MSG), allowing everyone to enjoy it liberally and conveniently. Eurocentric ignorance is your good fortune, because you know that maximizing umami is the key to successful chefdom.

2. ONE-UPSMANSHIP

From your time in the restaurant, you learned how people currently cook. Think about how it could be made better, often by increasing the umami, and then do it. That may sound easy. In fact, it is.

For example, every other restaurant in the city probably sells a chicken dish. Maybe they even brine it or salt it in advance. Let's say they have a roasted chicken breast; off the bat, you can cook it a bit less than they do, or better yet, use chicken thigh instead.

Or let's say they press a chicken thigh in a cast-iron skillet (resulting in crispy skin), you can one up them by ordering extra chicken skins (which cost next to nothing) and serving your thigh with five times as much of the delicious part.

But let's say someone has already done all of that. You can still do it better by adding one more umami element, like a slice of foie gras torchon or sea urchin. Or both. Remember, whatever other components you incorporate, the fast track to success runs through Oneupsburg with a pit-stop in Umamiville.

3. BUZZ

We've already discussed the importance of the Internet, but in case it wasn't clear, we were serious. You want people to talk about what you're doing, because aside from serving food so delicious that people talk about it, the quickest way to become successful is to serve food so noteworthy that people talk about it. Following the chicken train of thought, if a lot of places are serving chicken with a bread salad, then you should serve chicken with truffles steamed inside of a pig's bladder.

Or you can simply market the dish with a theme or a name. If you served the chicken thigh with additional crispy skin from the earlier example, it would already taste better than the chicken at the Park City Grill. People might talk about it. But if you called the dish "Silence of the Chickens—rooster in a hen suit with fava beans and a nice chianti reduction," people will blog about it.

4. VALUE

Unlike most chefs running stable kitchens trying to turn a profit, your main goal is to become successful. As such, since money is no object, you can make people happier by disregarding traditional food-cost models. Like we said, the faster you can eliminate any trace of what you learned in culinary school, the sooner you can get on the path to success. Rather than trying to have a food cost in the 25 percent range, simply organize your restaurant around not losing money. Allow your food cost to creep up to 30 percent, 50 percent, or 75+ percent. Whether your dish is $10 with a food cost of $2.50, or $20 with a food cost of $12.50, you will make the same amount of money. Plus you'll start to serve food that's more desirable than your competition in spite of disadvantages like transient staff, a shitty kitchen, and an unwelcoming dining room (if you're lucky enough to have one).

REAP YOUR REWARDS

Even with a shitty kitchen to work in and the Golden Rules in your pocket, you will need more help than you can anticipate. Get everyone you know to help—you don't have to reveal that your culinary dreams are about to swallow all their free time. Line up a friend with a truck. Email every food "journalist" in your city, but never have an actual conversation, because that leaves the door open to questions. You have no answers, so you might as well avoid their paltry concerns.

Next, get your hands on the right equipment. You may need to get married and have a wedding registry. A good start would be a powerful blender, which allows you to make anything into a sauce, purée, juice, velouté, fluid gel, or what-have-you. Second, you need a whipped-cream charger so you can turn any liquidy substance into a foam. You'll also need a deep fryer—still a reliable way to make food crispy and therefore popular. These three tools will transform a McDonald's double cheeseburger and fries into catnip for bloggers; your "Royale with Cheese" will comprise "savory meatloaf with potato tian, cheese mousse, and tomato-bread tuille" and the caller ID will say "The Food Network."

The night before you open to the public, take a shower and go to sleep early. This will be the last time your life feels under control. By the time you wake up, you'll already be a couple hours in the shit, no matter what time it is. Equipment will malfunction, food will be compromised, and the first-aid kit may or may not be adequate. Just carry on, and remember that no one in the dining room can taste your panic.

You are now at the pearly gates of the Promised Land. All you have left to do is spend an unholy amount of time in the kitchen and read about yourself on the Internet. Congratulations! Your rejection of money, a social life, or any conventional form of happiness is now complete. You are a successful chef.

We hope our heartfelt gratitude to everyone who made Mission Street Food possible, particularly our customers, comes through in this book. But we'd like to acknowledge a few individuals by name, too.

First, the business owners who took a chance on sharing their spaces with us: Justiniano and Juanita Gomez for their food cart, the Liang family for their restaurant, and Amanda and Howard Ngo for their grocery store. Our closest collaborators—Danny Bowien, Jason Fox, Xelina Leyba, Ian Muntzert, and Emma Sullivan—deserve both thanks for their partnership and praise for their outstanding talents.

The friends who became servers and the servers who became friends: Kea Anderson, Nikki Black, Tim Butler, Felix and Pedro Can, Ellie Cason, Chris Crawford, Vinny Eng, Alison Knight, Adam Koskoff, Sarah Kotcher, Logan Mitchell, Diana Nguyen, Julie Park, Jamie Riotto, Keli Rivers, Deb Tullman, and Kimberly Watson-Jew. Thanks to Youngmi Mayer for managing Mission Chinese Food, and thanks, too, to the former managers of Mission Street Food—Brendon Fox, Aubrey Hustead, and Sang Pahk—for their humor and flair.

The kitchen crew: Jesse Koide and all the staff at Mission Chinese Food, MSF interim sous-chef Matt Butler, emergency line cook Carlo Espinas, and volunteers Nicholas Chen, Sofia Leung, Kristine Low, Cindy Mojica, Ernesto Tanjuan, and Andrew Vlock.

During the first tumultuous days of MSF, we relied on the timely help of Eli Horowitz, Simon Huynh, Misao Kanda, Erin Klenow, and Angela Petrella; these friends stepped in to save the day before we could even ask for help, and we're grateful for it. Thanks to Vicky Myint and Steve Cook for their general support, and for devoting a large portion of their vacation to arduous work. Apologies to Jiyoun Chung, Nora Leibowitz, Karla Nielsen, and Sophia Wang for having to listen to us talk about MSF *all the time*. The LZA also provided unflagging support.

The guest chefs, without whom MSF would have been a lot less fun, if it existed at all: Collins Anderson, Lori Baker, Dontaye Ball, Nick Balla, Jeff Banker, David Barzelay, Bridget Batson, Eddie Blyden, Sylvan Mishima Brackett, Amy Marietta Brown, Matt Butler, Nick Castellanos, Ben Coe, Kirsten Dau, Jake Ersland, Azalina Eusope, John Farais, Ryan Farr, Roger Feely, Jean-Gabriel Ferrandon, Ted Fleury, Jesse Friedman, Paul Fromberg, Steven Gdula, Angela Gong, Mark Gravel, Jan-Henry Gray, Jordan Grosser, Tommy Halvorson, Bryan Harpel, Jeff Harpel, Tia Harrison, Leif Hedendal, Camille Jackson, Brandon Jew, Charlie Kleinman, Brandi Kozlowski, Chris Kronner, Amy Kurtz, Blake Kutner, Eddie Lau, Nicole LoBue, Timothy Luym, Russ Maclean, Ian Marks, Alex Marsh, Aaron Marthaler, Thomas Martinez, Sara Miles, James Moisey, Cindy Mojica, Douglas Monsalud, Richie Nakano, Corey Nead, Chad Newton, Christian Noto, Lauren O'Connor, Ryan Ostler, Jiwon Park, Iso Rabins, Jen Riate, Jeff Rosen, Veronica Salazar, Fred Sassen, Hugh Schick, Leonard Shek, Nick Spelletich, Mari Takahashi, Bud Teasley, Blair Warsham, Terri Wu, Noel Yin, and Katharine Zacher. Additional thanks go to the "phantom guest chefs" whose creations inspired us in the final days of MSF: Inaki Aizpitarte, Pascal Barbot, Massimo Bottura, Michel Bras, QuiQue DaCosta, Auguste Escoffier, David Everitt-Matthias, René Redzepi, and Tetsuya Wakuda. Thanks to Heston Blumenthal for the techniques we adapted from his series, *In Search of Perfection*.

The Bay Area food media: We got to know and admire the people behind several local blogs, including Jesse Friedman, Allan Hough, Mai Le, and John Oram. Jesse Friedman very generously allowed us to raid his archive of MSF photography for this book. Thanks as well to Sergio Ornelas, of the blog *GroceryEats.com*, for allowing us to reprint his review of an early night at Mission Street Food. We've also enjoyed seeing ourselves reflected in the writing of Internet journalists Carolyn Alburger, Lessley Anderson, John Birdsall, Marcia Gagliardi, Scott Hocker, Paolo Lucchesi, and Tamara Palmer—it's always fun to talk with them, and we've benefited from their opinions and advice more often than you'd think.

Many, many people provided additional help of all shapes and sizes: David Barzelay and Leiann Laiks offered legal advice, Marylou Jaso taught us about pastry, Dennis Kim was our business adviser and travel expert, Logan Mitchell signed us up for Twitter, Al Nguyen designed our website, Elizabeth Prueitt and Chad Robertson allowed us to use their kitchen, and Manita Jitngarmkusol designed a hilarious image of Anthony superimposed onto a Chinese Communist propaganda poster. We were fortunate enough to have beverages donated by DBI Inc., Elyse Winery, Matagrano Inc., Shoe Shine Wine, and Shmaltz Brewing. Many thanks are also due to the beneficiaries of our charitable giving, who publicized and attended our events in addition to already doing such great things for our community.

The people who helped us open Commonwealth: For starters, the customers who invested in the restaurant. Dante and Tracey Briones not only recognized the talents of Jason Fox, Xelina Leyba, and Ian Muntzert, but also wholeheartedly supported the charitable agenda we brought with us from MSF. Arleen and Robert Leibowitz provided an emergency loan with good humor and grace.

This book was a group effort, in matters both large and small. Chris Ying, our editor, first suggested the idea and saw it through every stage, from conceptualization to layout. Thanks go to everyone at McSweeney's who worked on the project, including Jordan Bass, Dave Eggers, Walter Green, Adam Krefman, Juliet Litman, Brian McMullen, Russell Quinn, and Michelle Quint.

Enormous thanks and admiration to Alanna Hale, who not only recorded the final days of MSF while she worked with us as a hostess but also photographed all of the step-by-step illustrations of our recipes, and many of the other pictures in this book. Alanna has stuck with us through some difficult and ridiculous circumstances, and her contributions go far beyond her invaluable photo-documentation.

Our greatest thanks are reserved for our families who contributed to this book directly or indirectly—in particular, Karen's parents and Anthony's *poa poa* helped develop our culinary sensibilities from a very young age. Special gratitude is due to Anthony's mother, Ellen Myint, for her invaluable help—she has used her talents as a CPA to do our taxes, her savvy as a businesswoman to advise us in our deals, and her Cantonese-language skills to negotiate on our behalf. She has done hours and hours of work without complaint or compensation, and she has cheered us on even when most people would have called us crazy. Without her, Mission Street Food would never have flourished in the way that it did. Thank you; this book is for you.

Additional MSF recipes, published by Food & Wine, *may be found online at:*
foodandwine.com/mission-street-food.

PHOTO CREDITS: *Recipe photos by Alanna Hale; archival MSF photos by Alanna Hale, Dennis Kim, Jesse Friedman, Jackson Solway, Simon Huynh, and John Oram; Mission Burger photos by Jason Adra; photograph of Noma musk-ox tartare by Food Snob.*

SAN FRANCISCO'S MISSION DISTRICT

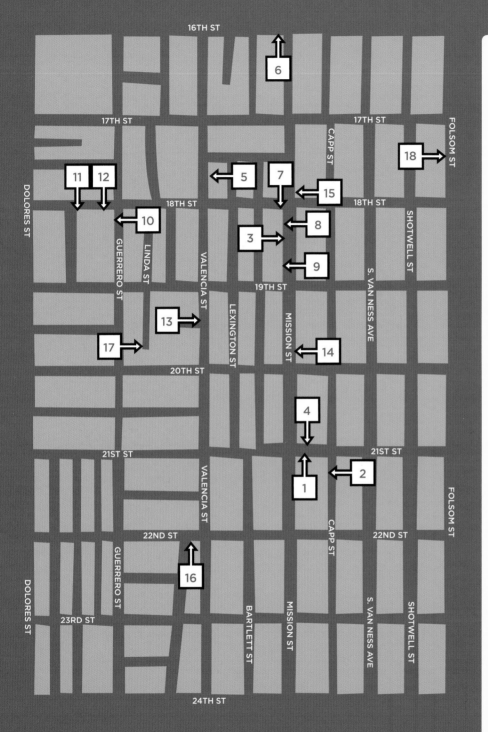

GENTRIFICATION INCREASES AS YOU TRAVEL WEST

PLACES PERTAINING TO MISSION STREET FOOD

1. Original MSF truck location (21st & Mission)
2. Karen and Anthony's apartment (Capp & 21st)
3. Mission Street Food/Lung Shan/Mission Chinese Food (2234 Mission)
4. Avalon Shop* (21st & Mission)
5. Bar Tartine (571 Valencia)
6. Antojitos Truck at BART station (16th & Mission)
7. Mission Burger/Duc Loi Market (2200 Mission)
8. Commonwealth (2224 Mission)
9. Taquería Cancún (2288 Mission)

FANCY PLACES

10. Tartine Bakery (600 Guerrero)
11. Bi-Rite (3639 18th)
12. Delfina/Delfina Pizzeria (3621, 3611 18th)
13. Range (842 Valencia)

STREET FOOD/POP-UP RESTAURANT HOSTS

14. Bruno's (2389 Mission)
15. La Esquina (2199 Mission)
16. Fabric8 (3318 22nd)
17. Casual Food Court* (19th & Linda)
18. Stable/Saison (2124 Folsom)

* No longer exists.

INDEX

RAT

You are imaginative, charming, and truly generous to the person you love. However, you have a tendency to be quick-tempered and overly critical. You are also inclined to be somewhat of an opportunist. Born under this sign, you should be happy in sales or as a writer, critic, or publicist. Some Rats: Shakespeare, Mozart, Churchill, Washington, Truman Capote.

BUFFALO

A born leader, you inspire confidence from all around you. You are conservative, methodical, and good with your hands. Guard against being chauvinistic and always demanding your own way. The Buffalo would be successful as a skilled surgeon, general, or hairdresser. Some Buffalos: Napoleon, van Gogh, Walt Disney, Clark Gable, Richard Nixon.

TIGER

You are sensitive, emotional, and capable of great love. However, you have a tendency to get carried away and be stubborn about what you think is right; often seen as a "Hothead" or rebel. Your sign shows you would be excellent as a boss, explorer, race car driver, or matador. Some Tigers: Marco Polo, Mary Queen of Scots, Dwight D. Eisenhower, Marilyn Monroe.

RABBIT

You are the kind of person that people like to be around; affectionate, obliging, always pleasant. You have a tendency, though, to get too sentimental and seem superficial. Being cautious and conservative, you are successful in business but would also make a good lawyer, diplomat, or actor. Some Rabbits: Rudolph Nureyev, Yakov Smirnoff, Confucius, Orson Welles, Einstein, Charo.

DRAGON

Full of vitality and enthusiasm, the Dragon is a popular individual even with the reputation of being foolhardy and a "big mouth" at times. You are intelligent, gifted, and a perfectionist but these qualities make you unduly demanding on others. You would be well-suited to be an artist, priest, or politician. Some Dragons: Joan of Arc, Pearl Buck, Bruce Lee, Freud.

SNAKE

Rich in wisdom and charm, you are romantic and deep thinking and your intuition guides you strongly. Avoid procrastination and your stingy attitude towards money. Keep your sense of humor about life. The Snake would be most content as a teacher, philosopher, writer, psychiatrist, and fortune teller. Some Snakes: Darwin, Edgar Allen Poe, Lincoln.

Location

The Restaurant will be located at 2234 Mission Street, San Francisco, CA 94110, inside an unpopular Chinese restaurant nestled between several Single Residence Occupancy buildings—lodging for individuals who can be described as "mentally unstable," "unhygienic," and "lowlifes." Said individuals will occasionally harass and disturb prospective diners. A few blocks away, at the 16th St. BART station, diners will be able to purchase "crack" cocaine.

Management Team

The Management will devote only partial attention to The Restaurant, and will be committed to separate full-time occupations.

Anthony Myint—a cook with no culinary education and no experience as a chef. He has never run a restaurant prior to opening The Restaurant.

Karen Leibowitz—a graduate student in the humanities with little interest or experience in the restaurant industry.

Marketing & Strategy

The Restaurant will not engage in any kind of mainstream promotion, such as permanent signage or a phonebook listing. The Restaurant will not have a phone number, and will filter telephonic communications through a Chinese-speaking message service.

The Restaurant's pricing model will require operation at maximum or extra-maximum capacity at all times. The Restaurant's successful operation will be contingent on Complete Strangers regularly preparing an amount of food commensurate with these expectations.

Unprofitable Agenda

If The Restaurant earns any profit, The Management will distribute it to unrelated nonprofit organizations.

The Restaurant will charge much less than nearby restaurants serving comparable food, and will pay significantly more per day for overhead than comparable restaurants.

Investment Analysis

All financing for the restaurant will be provided by The Management. The anticipated start up cost will be between $400 and $419, which will be invested primarily in pork belly and the rental of a "Guatemalan Snack Cart."

Return on Investment Analysis

In exchange for initial investments, The Management will receive a salary equivalent to an hourly rate far below minimum wage. The Management, selected staff, and friends will be allowed to eat food and drink beer at the expense of The Restaurant.